THE JOKER

THE JOKER

Twenty Years Inside The SAS

Pete Scholey

André Deutsch

First published in Great Britain in hardback in 1999
Published in paperback in 2002 by

André Deutsch
an imprint of the
Carlton Publishing Group
20 Mortimer Street
London
W1T 3JW

Reprinted in 2008, 2009

A catalogue record for this book is available from the British Library

ISBN 978-0-233-00205-7

Typeset by Derek Doyle & Associates, Liverpool
Printed and bound in the UK by
CPI Mackays, Chatham ME5 8TD

This book is dedicated to:

My wife, Carolyn, daughter Amy and son David whose undaunted love and support have guided me throughout my career and since.

CONTENTS

ACKNOWLEDGEMENTS

My thanks to Ingrid Connell, Andrew Lownie and Jack Hughes for their help and advice in editing and publishing *The Joker*.

Special thanks, too, to my friends Mark Howarth and Colin Wallace for their unfailing support and encouragement.

CHAPTER ONE

The Radfan mountains and the jungles of Borneo are a world away from where I grew up, and if you'd told me back then that I was going to be a career soldier for nearly thirty years, and that most of those years were going to be spent slogging around some of the wildest parts of the world, with a bergen on my back and a rifle in my hand, I'd have said you were mad. It just didn't happen to little lads like me from Brighton. We turned out like my dad: buying and selling, wheeling and dealing, doing whatever we could to keep the wolf from the door and the family together.

And what a family we were! I was number six out of eight children. Pat and Mary, my sisters, were the eldest; then came George; then Jean, another sister; then Tony, and then me. I appeared on 25 July 1936, born in the little flat above the corner grocery that Mum and Dad were then running. Nineteen thirty-six was a good year: Edward VIII was on the throne, briefly anyway; Fred Perry won the All England Lawn Tennis Championship at Wimbledon for the third year running; and the *Queen Mary* crossed the Atlantic on her maiden voyage to New York (funnily enough, I saw the real Queen Mary, mother of the King, a few years later in Brighton). When I was born, Mum and Dad were taking a

1

break from the family watercress business, which normally occupied my aunts and uncles, and several of my cousins as well.

It was a strange business, this watercress. It was grown near Chichester and then loaded onto a little train that chugged over to Brighton where the whole family got involved in sorting it, packing it and sending it off to our customers around the country. We didn't go as far as machine-gunning the competition, or putting horses' heads in their beds, but we were a kind of Mafia. Watercress was our thing, and you didn't mess with the Scholeys. Well, we were Catholics: we always had numbers on our side!

The first big event I can remember was the war: no surprise there. We were living in the Milner flats in Brighton by then and Dad went off to join up, leaving us six kids in the care of my mum (the last two boys were born after the war, but six was enough to be going on with).

Dad joined the RAF, and when he'd finished his basic training he was based at the Royal Naval Air Station at Ford. His job was to fly as crewman on the mail-runs going up to Scotland and back. He told me later that he used to spend every flight perched on this little seat behind his pilot, clutching a spanner in case anything went wrong with the plane. Not to fix it or anything like that: the cockpit of the plane was so small that they couldn't wear parachutes. They had to unclip their 'chute packs from the harness and store them in a rack, but it was only really possible to reach one of them easily. No, Dad wasn't going to fix the plane, he was going to fix the pilot: *thwack!*

One of Dad's early exploits happened soon after he'd joined up, when the German bombing of Britain was at its height. Heading back to his billet after a raid, he spotted a hole in the turf, put two and two together, and reported an unexploded bomb. All the accommodation was evacuated and they waited for some hours as the overworked bomb-disposal squad made their way through their nightly list of tasks. Mind you, it didn't take all that long for them to clear Dad's rabbit-hole. Well, it could have been dangerous – someone might have tripped over it in the dark.

Even though it was a tight squeeze for a family of eight, the great thing about being in Milner flats was that most of the rest of the family lived there as well, so my aunts and cousins were able to help out when they could. However, having such a lot to cope with got my mum down, and she had a miserable time. In one of my little flashes of memory from that time I can see her shaking with fright at the sound of the air-raid warning siren, before we were all bundled downstairs to the Anderson shelter next to my granny's flat on the ground floor.

Mum's fears weren't helped by all the horrible rumours that were going round: one of these claimed that any German bombers that hadn't dropped all their bombs on London would offload them over Brighton on their way home. Another – even more frightening – maintained that the Germans thought that our block of flats, and the one next to it, was a barracks, and that Hitler had ordered a special raid to destroy them. Neither of these stories was true, of course, and we weren't ever directly bombed, but they were just about believable, and they were certainly enough to contribute to the panic of civilians who only wanted to protect their families against the threat of the Luftwaffe.

But even though Hitler never did score a direct hit on the Scholeys, he came very close. When I was about four or five years old, I was at home one day after my brothers and sisters had gone off to school. I was sitting on the big old brass bed that the five youngest of us slept in, playing with

3

my toy cars and planes, when a bomb hit the clinic next to the flats, not more than thirty or forty yards from where I was. Most of the people inside it were killed or badly injured, and the blast brought down several nearby buildings, and damaged many others, of which ours was one.

I have a very vivid memory of a loud bang, and looking up to see the entire window, frame, glass and all, coming straight towards me. I had the sensation of being lifted bodily from the bed, thrown against the wall and falling to the floor. After that, I only recollect lying there, and the feeling that I couldn't move.

Sometime later an ARP warden found me, trapped beneath a wardrobe covered with wreckage and debris. Many years later I learned from my mother that I did not cry out, which is why it took some time to locate me. The wardrobe had fallen onto the bed, creating a small sheltered space and saving me from the falling rubble. Next day I stood with Mum and a big group of neighbours looking at one of the destroyed buildings lying in ruins in front of us, listening to them discussing how a man had been decapitated by a panel of corrugated iron blasted from the roof. As I scuffed my feet in the dust and rubble, I found a sixpenny piece. I didn't think about it then but I suppose it belonged to one of the people who had been killed or injured. Nearly sixty years later it remains a powerful memory.

Dad was given thirty-six hours' compassionate leave and arrived home in the evening, looking strong and handsome in his RAF uniform with its brightly polished brass badges and buttons. As soon as he walked in, he picked me up and gave me a big bear hug. He used to wear one of those side-hats decorated with an RAF badge, and he would let me put it on. Then I would bury my face in it and smell the Brylcreem from his hair (still pretty much obligatory in the RAF, even now). When he was away, I missed him terribly, as we all did, but sometimes I would catch that smell – clean hair, Brylcreem and an RAF side-hat – and it was as if he was there with me. It still happens from time to time.

Around this time, a great big low-loader parked outside the Dome in Brighton, carrying the wreckage of a German bomber. This was quite an attraction for the few hours it was there and I, along with most of the other small boys in the area, spent some time staring at it. Funnily enough, a couple of years ago I was looking at a book, *Sussex at War*, which featured a photograph of this scene and I'm sure if it was enlarged you would be able to see the small short-trousered Scholey lurking in the crowd. A few weeks after the appearance of the bomber my sister Mary took me with her on a mission to buy a couple of pence-worth of bacon bones for my mum to make into soup. As we walked along the main road, we heard a roar and looked up to see two German planes zooming past so low we could see the pilots' faces. They weren't going to shoot us or anything but Mary had the presence of mind to pull me back into a shop doorway just in case.

The bombing of the clinic made my mum decide that it would be better to get us out of Brighton for the summer and so she took us all off hop-picking near Goudhurst in Kent. Well, that's not quite accurate: she picked the hops, earning eightpence a bushel, while us kids played about. Still, at least we were out of harm's way in the countryside, sleeping on straw in a barn and eating food cooked on big twig fires.

One incident remains in my mind from this summer. One morning a German bomber came over very low, trailing smoke from both engines and obviously badly shot up. I ran out of the barn with the other kids to see what would happen and promptly collided with the legs of a big, fat lady carrying a bowl of boiling hot water, which she spilled all down my back. My sister Jean took me up to the first-aid post (where they also used to make pies, for some strange reason) and they fixed me up so well I was left without a mark on me.

Jean was a resourceful girl. One of the biggest problems for us kids in wartime was the shortage of sweets because of rationing. One solution was to hang around the American soldiers who began to appear around 1942, because they always had plenty of chewing gum and Hershey bars to hand out if you asked them nicely, and my older sister Pat used to go out with an American, so that was handy. Jean was more systematic, though.

For some reason, a lot of cancelled ration coupons used to be dumped on one of the municipal tips round Brighton and Jean discovered that some of them were in good enough nick to be cleaned up, dyed to the colour of the month, then used in the gloomy little sweet shop just across from where we lived. It was run by an old boy who was too short-sighted to see what we'd done.

Despite the rationing, I don't ever remember being hungry or going short of food as a kid. Dad used to send little parcels home: stuff he pinched from the cookhouse, I expect. And the family made sure that us kids had enough to eat. At that time, we were allowed one fresh egg a week which we'd have for tea on Sunday afternoon, but often I'd ask Mum for my Sunday egg a couple of days early, and usually she would give it to me. Despite this, every Sunday I'd still have an egg in my egg-cup and it took a long time for me to work out how this was possible: of course, Mum was giving me hers.

We wouldn't be cold either. Five of us kids slept in one big bed, and in the winter, as well as the blankets, Mum would pile all the coats in the house on top of us, from her own overcoat to the little baby's jackets, and although most of them had rolled off by the morning, it got us off to a nice warm start.

I suppose the arrival of the Americans signalled the beginning of the end of the war. I remember just before D-day, when I was eight years old, seeing all these trucks parked along the seafront, nose to tail, stretching as far as the eye could see. Some of us smaller kids tried walking along the top of them, jumping from truck to truck to see how far we could get without putting our feet on the ground. Some of the older boys reckoned you'd be able to get all the way to Hastings. But then, a few days later, they were all gone; and many of the happy, smiling GIs who'd joked with us and given us their chocolate bars were dead in the dunes of Omaha beach and the hedgerows of Normandy.

Only a couple of months later, we all heard a strange rumbling sound and rushed out to watch wave after wave of Dakotas, some towing gliders, as well as their fighter escorts, heading off – as we later discovered – to the Arnhem catastrophe. I was too small to realize it at the time, but I expect that this close proximity to the war – and for nearly five years, if you lived on the south coast, you were pretty much on the front line – later made it seem natural to me that I should follow a military career, or, at least, serve in the armed forces.

When the war came to an end and Dad came home there was no great song and dance. My sister Pat had eventually married a Canadian soldier called Robbie, and had a baby, and when he was demobilized she went back to Canada with him. Being good Catholics, though, Mum and Dad didn't let the grass grow under their feet and there were soon more children on the way.

Sadly, when Pat left, it was the last time I ever saw her. Twenty years later she came back to see the family, and they had a big party, but I was away on operations in Aden and I missed it. Unbeknownst to all of us, she was suffering from cancer by then and died before I could get to see her again.

We were all pleased to have Dad back because we've always been a very close and loving family, but he wasn't the sort of man to want to dwell on what he'd been through. As far as he was concerned, he'd done his bit and that was the end of it. He threw his uniform away, and didn't bother to apply for any campaign medals, as far as I remember. Then he began to look around for some way of supporting his large brood. The watercress business had been sold when all the male Scholeys joined up so he needed to find something new.

Although nobody was being killed any more, the end of the war didn't change things a lot. Winston Churchill had lost the election and left office, making Mr Attlee the Prime Minister, but for one reason or another the Labour government clung on to rationing and lots of the rules that had come with the war, like conscription, so there was still an atmosphere of emergency and regulation, as well as a thriving black economy. Being the kind of chap he was, this was where Dad scented success.

One thing I remember about Dad coming back from the war was the large roll of banknotes he was carrying – well, it seemed a lot to me at the time – which I suppose must have been a combination of savings and a gratuity. And this provided the float for his first enterprise: unlicensed bookmaking.

Being the sort of family we were, it wasn't surprising that we all got involved. Dad's office was in my gran's flat downstairs, and my role was to act as a runner, getting the cash and betting slips squirrelled away in case of a police raid. Soon after he started, Dad gave me a good piece of advice, which I can't say I've always stuck to but which has always seemed sensible. He was doing his accounts at the end of one day, getting ready to do his round of paying out to the successful punters, and he showed me two piles of money.

'Son, this pile is what I owe to all the winners who've had a bet with me today, and this one is my money. Now, which one's bigger?'

'Your money, Dad.'

'Exactly son. You can't beat the odds, that's why I'm in the business.'

But, of course, he wasn't for very long. In a small town like Brighton the police soon got to hear about what he was up to, and while he never got caught in the act, their interest persuaded him to try his hand at something else, and he started selling fruit and veg off a barrow.

In those days you were allowed to set up on any street corner up to ten in the morning and then you had to move on. But provided that you were moving, you were okay, and this gave the rest of us yet another part to play in his business. Dad would be up at four in the morning and down the market, looking for nice cheap stuff to sell on. Then we would spend an hour or so helping him get the barrow set up and nicely arranged and he was off, racing the other barrow boys for the best pitch. Once he was started, we would come into our own, acting as lookouts, watching out for the shiny silver decoration on top of the policemen's helmets as they made their way through the crowds.

But the fruit and veg business was pretty cut-throat with so much competition about, and certainly not the most secure way of bringing up a family, so Dad's next step was to set up as a totter, a kind of rag and bone man, pushing his barrow around town collecting all sorts of old rubbish and sorting it out so that he could sell it on. He'd get eightpence for a trilby hat; sixpence for a rabbit skin; a halfpenny each for jam jars; a few pence for a pound of white wool, and so on.

Meanwhile, I'd started my education at St John the Baptist Secondary Modern, our local Catholic school and the place you were sent if you'd failed your eleven-plus exam, like I had. It was now that I first encountered a problem that was, in some ways, to shape my life. Back in the 1940s there was no mucking about with 'child-centred education' and the nuns who taught us were strict and unrelenting. I had no problem with reading and writing, but for reasons that I couldn't then explain, figures meant nothing to me. If I looked at a page of sums, after a couple of seconds the numbers on the page would seem to swim around, as if I was looking at a jigsaw with the pieces all jumbled up, and I couldn't see any way of putting them back together.

Well, nowadays 'dyscalculia' is a recognized condition, related to dyslexia. But in those days, as far as my teachers were concerned, it was because I was thick and not trying hard enough. My own reaction made things worse. Frustrated by my inability to do the work, I resorted to pratting about, with the result that I spent so long standing in the corner, I knew all the spiders by their first names.

Being the class clown is all very well, but after a while nobody wants to know you, and I ended up as something of a loner and also, I'm ashamed to admit, a little bit of a bully. I was helped in this by the fact that the only sport I was any good at was boxing. My two mates were the other two class dunces, Rudolf Syfflet (not the best surname for a schoolboy) and George Geady, and we got our laughs from coming out of school at lunch time, walking down the main street and taking the mickey out of everybody in sight. Even between ourselves we behaved stupidly. One time I was winding George up by slapping him on the legs below his shorts, and he responded by pushing me over, picking up half a brick and thumping me on the head with it. As if that wasn't bad enough, I took a swing back at him and managed to splatter his nose halfway across his face. That dropped both of us in the shit and we were soon in front of the teacher, getting six of the best across the backs of our knuckles with a big metal ruler.

Now a clip round the ear or a rap on the knuckles is understandable if you've been fighting, but what used to get me down was the beltings I'd get when I couldn't do the work. We'd be sitting there in rows at our little wooden desks, scratching away with the old-fashioned dip pens, or in my case staring at the big inky blot that had formed on my exercise book. Then the teacher would come up behind and *thwack*! In wintertime, I would spend the rest of the day with my knuckles in my mouth or under my arms, rocking backwards and forwards, crying and giggling at the same time, trying to make the pain go away.

We even got a clout for missing church. We had Mass every Wednesday at school, but if you missed it on a Sunday, you had to bring a note in from your parents to explain why. The old Irish priest would come around on Monday morning, and if he suspected you hadn't shown up, you'd go through his own little version of the catechism: 'Were you at Mass on Sunday?' 'Which church did you go to?' 'Who took the Mass?' 'Scholey you're a bloody liar! Get outside the door.' *Thwack!*

But I was saved from all this by one of the few teachers I came across who had any time for me. Mr Liddle was a history teacher who'd been in the Royal Flying Corps in the First World War and had decided, just after the Second World War had finished, to set up an Air Training Corps unit at our school. Mr Liddle saw that I was never going to be an academic superstar, but he also recognized that I lacked confidence and a focus for my life, and that was what the ATC provided. Once a week, we would put on our uniforms, and go and do a little drill, followed by something like first-aid training, or aircraft recognition, and then a few team games or sports. Not much perhaps, but better than hanging around on the streets getting into trouble.

One of the highlights of the year was the Shoreham Air Display, where we would act as guides and runners on the airfield. In the run-up to the display, my unit became involved in selling tickets and programmes, and seeing my enthusiasm, Mr Liddle would let me out of school an hour early so that I could go home, put on my uniform and make a start on my sales campaign.

One summer this became a sort of obsession for me. I'd leave the school at three and then walk from Rottingdean as far as Hove or even Shoreham itself, calling in at the big hotels, knocking on doors and flogging the programmes at a shilling a go. When the display finally arrived, I'd sold over 800 programmes and my reward was promotion to acting corporal and my first ever flight in an old Avro Anson, all the way from Shoreham, round Beachy Head and back. Well, that was that for me. I knew what I wanted to do with my life. I wanted to be in aircrew.

I suppose I was only about fourteen at this point, but I went to see Mr Liddle and told him that I had decided to volunteer for the Royal Air Force. Although he told me that he didn't think I was ready for it, he agreed that I should have a go. Then I told my dad, who was all for it, and finally I went off to get the forms from the RAF recruiting office.

A couple of weeks later saw me at the RAF College at Cosford for my initial selection for a twelve-year RAF apprenticeship. I'm sorry to say that I lasted four hours. I sat in front of a series of test papers, and they stared back at me, and that was it. I couldn't do them, so home I went. I slunk into the house and told Dad, and he was very nice about it, but I was struck with the thought, 'What am I going to do now?'

The answer was to try again. A year or so later I volunteered for adult service starting at the age of sixteen, and once more I went off for my assessment, this time at the old airship base at Cardington, which by then had been converted into a recruiting station. I did better this time – I managed to last a whole day – but my scores in the tests were hopeless, even though I'd lowered my sights and was only trying to obtain a basic three-year engagement. It began to dawn on me that I was never going to make it into the Royal Air Force.

But, of course, this was the beginning of the 1950s, and although I might not be going to join the Royal Air Force, I was going to have to do my National Service when I got to the age of eighteen, and in the meantime I needed to find work and earn some money. Looking back, I'm amazed at how many jobs I had over the next two years. I dug holes for the Borough Surveyor; I dug holes for the Electricity Board; I dug holes for the Gas Board; I baked bread; I delivered bread; I delivered newspapers; I was a plasterer's mate; I was a builder's labourer. All in all, more than thirty different jobs in less than two years.

Next time you pass through Gatwick Airport, you can console yourself with the fact that I spent four days working there for my brother-in-law, pushing a barrow full of cement through the muddy building site and unloading bricks from the back of a truck, with eyes full of brick-dust and fingers blunted like hammerhead sharks. And if you live in the early housing estates in Crawley, I helped build those as well.

But all the time I was doing these crummy jobs, I was hating it: none of them lasted more than a few weeks and some were only a couple of days. My drifting did finally lead to some tension with my family who had understandably begun to think of me as a bit of a waster. By now Dad had acquired a proper pitch and was back to selling fruit and veg, and doing quite well, but I think he was keen that we should all settle down and stand on our own feet as soon as possible. I knew that I was set on a career in the military but my record so far didn't necessarily indicate that I was going to be able to stick with it. Still, it passed the time until the fateful day when the little brown envelope plopped through the letterbox 'On Her Britannic Majesty's Service' to tell me that my attendance would shortly be required at a National Service medical board.

I had a choice. Either I could wait for my appointment and go with the flow, or I could take myself down to the local recruiting office and volunteer, thus short-cutting the whole procedure, and that's what I did.

It wasn't plain sailing, though. The recruiting centre for the army was at the Oddfellows' Hall in Brighton, where I signed all the forms and then had a medical, which was where the snag arose. This strange collection of half-dead looking doctors weighed, measured, prodded and probed before pronouncing me 'grade three' and a borderline case, because of a scarred eardrum. I did my best to persuade them and eventually they agreed that, as I was a volunteer, they would give me the benefit of the doubt.

So there I was, eighteen years old and off to join the army.

Chapter Two

I don't suppose that joining the army as an eighteen-year-old National Serviceman in the mid-1950s was all that different from joining the army nowadays. It's a huge culture shock, of course, but at the same time it's a ritual that every soldier who has ever joined the British Army has been through, and although there have been some superficial changes, I don't imagine that much of it would come as a surprise to someone joining up in the year 2000 either.

I and about forty other ill-assorted herberts rolled up at the Royal Army Service Corps camp at Blandford in Dorset and straight away we were into the swing of it. Doubled over to our accommodation: eighteen-man rooms in wooden huts; a steel bedframe and a locker to call our own; a stove with a coal fire to keep the place warm.

Then *wham*! Doubled to the barber – Paddy the Chop – out come the clippers: *zhmm zhmm zhmm*. Suddenly I've only got an eighth of an inch of hair left. Then doubled over to the clothing store for: battledress, two sets; big leather-soled and studded ammunition boots, two pairs, 1937 pattern webbing, a great collection of canvas straps covered in ominous-looking brass buckles, together with berets, duffel bags, PT kit and a hundred and one other things that I would never have imagined I needed, but now found I did.

Then back to the accommodation to find out how you put it all on.

If, like me, you'd come from a working-class background where money was short but, at the same time, had experienced the fierce discipline of a Roman Catholic secondary school, then the shock to the system wasn't too severe. One feature of National Service – one of the better ones in my view – was that it was a melting pot. You got kids like me, you got lads who'd been at public schools and you got some people who'd been at university. You also had a selection of villains and nutcases as well – people who didn't want to be there and had no intention of knuckling down and making the best of it. In the first few weeks we had people trying to hang themselves in the bogs, we had people drink cans of Brasso in an attempt to poison themselves and one evening I watched a lad cut all of his kit into postage-stamp-sized pieces with a pair of scissors. On the other hand, a lot of these conscripts were magnificent, and you only had to look at the success of the British troops who fought in Korea, Kenya, Malaya and elsewhere during the fifties to see that the majority were just as good as any other soldiers Britain has produced in the last fifty years.

One of the big features of life during our first twelve weeks of basic training, apart from all the square-bashing, weapon training and so forth, was the amount of time we spent cleaning, ironing and polishing our kit. You still hear soldiers complaining about this today, of course, but I can assure you that this is an area where there has been a big improvement. Take boots, for example: when I joined, the standard boot for British soldiers was what was called the 'ammunition boot'. This was a sturdy ankle-length, black leather design, which also featured leather soles into which were hammered steel studs to improve their grip. In a perfect world, this kind of boot, although old-fashioned even in those days, could be made supple and waterproof by being regularly dubbined or polished. In combination with the canvas gaiters we wore, it would have been perfectly effective for general field-soldiering. Unfortunately, this kind of common-sense approach was unthinkable. Instead, we all had to go through the ritual of 'bulling' to try to achieve a perfect mirror-like shine all over our best boots, and on the toes and heels of our everyday pair. The first 'problem' with the boots was that the leather they were made from was covered in little tiny pimples, and to get a mirror finish the leather needs to be smooth. This was achieved by heating the handle of a metal teaspoon over a candle and using it to press the pimples flat. Of course, applying red-hot teaspoons to it is not really conducive to preserving the leather for extended use, but never mind. The next step was to coat the boot liberally in Kiwi polish, allow it to dry, and then repeat the process until the whole boot was covered with a smooth, thick layer. Finally, with a clean, damp duster, you gently apply tiny quantities of polish in a circular motion, polishing the layer of polish, rather than the actual leather, thus achieving a shiny surface in which you can, literally, see the reflection of your face.

Of course, at the same time as you achieve the ultimate shiny boot, you are also ruining it for anything other than parades, guard duties and so forth, when a high degree of bullshit is required. It's all very well to look smart but I wonder if it's worth, in effect, destroying kit to do so. A friend of mine, who had served in Korea, later told me how, after several weeks hard soldiering in their 'field' boots, members of the Glosters had only their best boots to change into when their first pair began to wear out, and as soon as these were exposed to field conditions, they fell to pieces: bad news when you have half the Chinese People's Liberation Army on your tail!

With our webbing equipment, the problem was slightly different. All the belts, straps, pouches and packs were made out of a sort of yellowy-green cotton canvas material which looked horrible in its raw state and absorbed water, mud and filth like a sponge. The army's solution to this was blanco, a green paste you applied to the webbing which made it a uniform colour. Well, again, it did make everything look smarter, but I have to say it would have been easier if they had adopted the obvious solution they worked out a few years later, and simply dyed everything the colour they wanted to achieve in the first place.

After the initial basic training I moved on to begin to learn my trade with the Royal Army Service Corps. The RASC, which subsequently became the Royal Corps of Transport and is now the Royal Logistics Corps, was responsible for moving all of the army's heavy equipment and stores to wherever they were required, whether by land, sea or air. There were, and still are, plenty of units in the Corps that do the exotic stuff – air despatching, maritime operations, and so on – but I was a truck driver, pure and simple. I learned how to drive on a 3-ton Bedford, and soon had experience on a broad range of now forgotten military vehicles: the Austin Champ; the Willys Jeep; the Stalwart; you name it, I drove it. And that, broadly speaking, is how I spent my National Service: ferrying men and equipment round the training areas, camps and garrisons of the south of England.

I came out of the RASC as a qualified military driver with a £70 gratuity, a railway warrant home and the determination to re-enlist in the army as soon as possible. I went home to

Brighton, spent a couple of weeks staying with my family then took myself down to the recruiting office to sign up again. I'd enjoyed myself in the RASC, but I was pretty sure now that I was ready to move on, and this time I fancied a crack at something difficult: I wanted to join the Guards.

I'm not sure if I entirely remember why I wanted to do this, but it certainly had something to do with the smart uniforms and cheese-cutter caps they wore. That sounds silly now, but I was still in the grip of a complex about my wasted schooling, and I wanted to show people, and my family most of all, that I could hack it.

Unfortunately for me, with National Service in full swing, the army wasn't short of private soldiers, as the recruiting sergeant informed me. While he promised he would try his best, he couldn't guarantee to get me into a Guards regiment. Well, that's what he told me anyway, and I certainly believed him. Two or three days later, I returned to the office to be told that there were no vacancies in the Guards but that he could get me into the Royal Regiment of Artillery. The Gunners.

I thought about this for a few moments and decided, 'Yeah, that'll do me nicely.' Although, I'd just spent eighteen months as an RASC driver, I was still pretty naïve. I didn't have a clue what the Gunners were about, but it sounded all right, and pretty soon I was signing the forms for a three-year engagement and collecting another rail warrant to take me to Park Hall Camp in Oswestry.

Basic training in the RASC wasn't easy, but I tell you, for the first sixteen weeks in the Royal Artillery my arse didn't touch the ground. Even though I was supposedly a trained soldier, I started at the beginning again, spending the first four weeks square-bashing as a member of 148 Meiktila Battery (which is now a highly specialized commando forward observation unit but was then a recruit training unit) and then going on for continuation training at Kimmel Park Camp in Rhyl, north Wales.

Once again I was selected as a driver and went through another training course with Royal Artillery instructors, but I was also trained as a crewman on the old 25-pounder field gun and on the 5.5 inch heavy anti-aircraft gun, just for good measure. Finally, at the end of this second bout of basic training, I was posted back to Oswestry as a member of the newly formed 27 Guided Weapons Regiment, Royal Artillery.

The arrival of nuclear weapons and ballistic missiles at the end of the Second World War had a profound effect on military thinking. For a while, it seemed as if the Americans' possession of the atom bomb made them more or less invulnerable to attack from the Soviet Union, which had begun shaping up as the only credible enemy almost as soon as the Germans were beaten in 1945. But then the Soviets got their nasty hands on nuclear weapons as well and the arms race started. As part of the British response to all this, 27 Regiment was designed to use tactical guided missiles in the event of a Soviet invasion of Europe.

It had been decided that, because we were going to be one of the first two guided-weapons regiments in the British Army, they would trawl the rest of the Royal Artillery to find the best drivers, the best signallers, the best mechanics, and so on, to staff it. That was the idea anyway. Whenever the army decides to do something like this, the response is always the same: everyone agrees, 'What a good idea!' and then all the drongoes, deadheads and weirdos who've not got past the rank of Gunner for fifteen years suddenly get a promotion to Lance Bombardier and a posting into whichever new 'élite' is being formed.

Still, they weren't a bad bunch of lads and I had a good time with the regiment. My first big trip away with them was to the missile range at Benbecula on South Uist in the Outer Hebrides. I was part of a team sent to St Kilda with monitoring gear to track the course of the missiles. The first time that the missiles – an American design called the 'Corporal' – were fired, they'd gone all over the place, the reason being that they'd placed them on concrete launch pads, which caused vibration when the rocket motor fired. In these tests they were fired from sand, which caused no such problems.

After three months of tests we returned to Oswestry for the regiment to begin the process of working up to operational readiness and eventual deployment in Germany. Before this happened we made a temporary move to Crookham camp near Aldershot in Hampshire, and from there we took part in build-up training: exercising on Salisbury Plain and the other training areas of the south of England.

But, as it happened, I didn't accompany the regiment to Germany. One of the many British Army formations which was then based around 'the Shot' was the 16th Parachute Brigade: Britain's airborne forces.

The focus of 16 Parachute Brigade was, of course, the battalions of the Parachute Regiment who formed the main striking force within it, but it also included the supporting arms: Engineers, Signals, Gunners, as well as services like doctors, cooks, bottlewashers, and so on, all of whom had to be Para-trained. Being based at Crookham brought me into contact with 33 Parachute Light Regiment Royal Artillery and so, with around a year of my contract left to run, and by now a bombardier (the Artillery equivalent of a corporal), I decided that I needed a more adventurous challenge and volunteered for service with the airborne forces.

Most armies don't get too fussed about parachute training: if you're daft enough to volunteer to do it, you get a quick physical check (though it's always struck me that a mental one might be more appropriate), you do your parachute training and that's it: you're airborne. Somehow, though, the British Army could never do things that simply. Instead we had the whole process of P Company to get through.

P Company is a series of tests designed to check out the airborne volunteer's fitness and determination before he gets on to the serious business of parachuting. Basically you turn up at the airborne forces depot, you're given a great big rucksack and a few other bits of kit and then spend the next three weeks charging around with said rucksack, now filled to weigh thirty-five pounds, firmly attached to your back. The tests included forced marches, assault courses, stretcher races and milling, where we all punched the living daylights out of each other while the instructors checked for suitable signs of aggression. As all the lads started mixing it – and some really knew how to box – I found it best to drop to the floor and bite ankles. Equally unpopular was the trainasium, a rickety scaffolding frame designed to see if you wet your pants when faced with heights. And it's only at the end of this that you're actually allowed to go off and do the parachuting!

As well as P Company, transferring to the airborne gunners also meant retraining on the specialist guns and equipment they used, and particularly the lightweight 105-mm Pack Howitzer, and it was while I was doing this that my contract came to its end. In the normal course of events the process of re-enlistment would be a formality, particularly for a junior NCO like me who was obviously keen on a long-term military career, but in truth I was having doubts. I went in front of the commanding officer for an interview and laid my cards on the table.

'Bombardier Scholey, have you decided whether you want to continue to serve with the Royal Regiment?'

'I've made my decision, sir, and I would like to leave.'

'What? Why on earth do you want to go now? You haven't even done your para course yet . . . '

'Sir, the thing is, I don't want to be a parachute gunner, I want to be a thoroughbred. I want to join the Parachute Regiment itself.'

As you can imagine, that went down like a fart in a space-suit and I had an uncomfortable few days. You can't blame them: almost everyone in the army is convinced that their regiment or corps is the only place to be and they were most likely astonished that I wanted to go elsewhere. Still, there you go.

Being based in Aldershot, demob presented me with an easy choice. I walked down Queen's Avenue from North Camp to the Parachute Regiment Depot, presented myself at the gate, explained what I wanted, signed on and, as luck would have it, joined a squad starting their basic training that same day.

Of course, by now I'd actually spent the best part of five years in the army and although there were a few problems of adjustment – the Paras did foot drill slightly differently from the way I'd been taught, for example – the basics were second nature to me. After a couple of weeks, the squad officer, Lieutenant Peacock, sent for me and told me: 'Scholey, it's ridiculous you doing all this again. You know your stuff with the weapons. So we're moving you up a squad.'

This was excellent news: now all I had to do to pass out as a member of the regiment and go to an operational squad was learn some infantry tactics, get through the battle camp at Brecon and the parachute course. All parachute training in the British forces is run by the RAF, and back in the late fifties the parachute school was at RAF Abingdon near Oxford. Coming after a week of being screamed at on P

Company, the parachuting was a bit like a holiday. Provided you turned up on time and were properly dressed, nobody gave you a hard time. You did the work and then off down the Naafi in the evening for a couple of pints followed by bed. The early part of the course went through all the various techniques for fitting and adjusting the parachutes and equipment, exiting from the aircraft, steering the parachute in the air, landing, rolling, and getting sorted out again. We also learned what happened when you got a serious malfunction in your parachute: you whistled in and hit the ground very hard.

I enjoyed the battle camp as well, even though it was, I think, the toughest training I'd ever done. The great thing about the Parachute Regiment was that it didn't muck around. It was a regiment that prided itself on being ready to go at any time and this meant you had to work hard, but we played hard as well and I had a great time. There are some funny ideas going around about what the Paras do. An old colleague of mine, in a book he wrote, describes them as 'shock troops', as if that was a special role that they've been given, but I think he's wrong. Although the original Paras were descended from the wartime army commandos, by the time they'd earned their battle honours in Tunisia, at D-day and at Arnhem, their role had changed and they were essentially a light infantry force capable of being delivered by parachute. So when I passed out of the Airborne Forces Depot at Aldershot, proudly wearing my maroon beret with the Parachute Regiment badge and cloth wings of a qualified military parachutist, I was proud to be a member not of some kamikaze shock squad, but the best airborne infantry regiment the world has ever seen.

There are three regular battalions in the Parachute Regiment: 1 Para never seem to go anywhere, and they're known as the 'Home Guard'; 3 Para were the drinking battalion; I was posted to 2 Para, the drill pigs (instructors). A couple of days after passing out of the depot, I joined the troopship TT *Dunera* and sailed for Cyprus, for my first overseas posting.

Between 1954 and 1959 Cyprus was the scene of a fierce guerrilla war between Greek Cypriot EOKA terrorists and the British colonial authorities. The Greeks wanted Cyprus to be unified with mainland Greece, and as they made up 80 per cent of the population you could see they had a point, but oddly enough the 20 per cent Turkish population didn't agree. Instead the Turkish Cypriots wanted reunification with Turkey, which had ruled the island before the British takeover at the turn of the century. As it happened, us Brits had been keen to hang on to the place for ourselves, seeing it as a key strategic base for our operations in the Middle East.

The upshot of all this was that the Greeks had imported Colonel George Grivas, a Greek Nationalist extremist, and he had set up EOKA, which had spent several years bumping off Turks and Brits in roughly equal numbers. Fortunately, all this was quietening down by the time I arrived to join A Company of 2 Para and reported to their camp just outside Limassol.

Cyprus has changed a lot in the forty years since I first arrived there. Although it was in the process of becoming independent, it remained undivided at that time and in many ways retained a kind of British veneer, despite the splendid Mediterranean backdrop. I wasn't exactly a fresh-faced squaddie when I turned up – I'd been in the army for five years after all – but I knew enough to work out that the best way to settle in would be to keep my head down for the first few months and play the grey man, even though I knew, with my sense of humour, that this was not going to be easy.

The first problem arose when I was given the job of rounding up and shooting the stray dogs that infested the camp. I've always liked animals, but these things were horrible: scabby, mangy, often half blind and riddled with all sorts of diseases, they hung around the open-sided cookhouse marquee, stealing food and scraps, fighting and making a nuisance of themselves. I was sent out with a pair of thick gauntlets, some rope to tie them up, a 9mm Browning pistol and a box of rounds to thin them out. After a hard morning chasing the buggers around, I'd got a bunch of them in a gully outside the camp, which we used as a tip, and went through the grim business of shooting them with a round to the back of their heads, between their ears which, if nothing else, is the quickest way to do it.

Having shot the dogs we then set about burning the bodies in a big heap, after soaking them with petrol. With this done, we were making our way back to the camp when we saw another one, a great big fucker this time, and with some trepidation we enticed it down to the tip where I did the necessary – and threw it on the fire.

The company was on guards and duties this week so I had various other tasks to do before I headed back to the guardroom to hand in the pistol. When I arrived there, the provost sergeant was waiting.

'Scholey, you need to get your arse up to the RSM's office right now!'

'Okay, Sar'nt, but why?'

'Just get up there, at the double!'

I doubled over to the RSM's, wondering what the hell I'd done. Arriving outside, I reported to the clerk then heard a big voice booming: 'Is that Scholey? Get in here.'

I formed up in front of the RSM's desk.

'Scholey, you realize you're in the shit? We've had to send for Pierrepoint.'

Pierrepoint was the hangman who'd just retired after topping the best part of 500 victims.

'Why, sir, what have I done?'

'It's murder, Scholey. You've shot the Devon and Dorsets' mascot!'

'Fuck me!'

'Don't tempt me, sonny! It's a corporal and they're holding a regimental funeral for it this afternoon.'

The Devon and Dorsets were in the camp below us and, as it happened, their mascot was an English bull mastiff which they allowed to wander round their patch. A series of complicated phone calls managed to persuade the D and D's hierarchy that it was an honest mistake and no action was taken.

But battalion-level diplomacy failed to convince the D and D's soldiery that they weren't the victims of Para brutality and revenge was planned. A three-man fighting patrol of Devon and Dorsets was despatched the next night on a mission to assassinate our mascot, Bruneval, a Shetland pony.

Most people think of Shetland ponies as sweet little things that children can happily learn to ride on and which wouldn't say boo to a goose. Wrong. Bruneval was a vicious little bastard – Para trained – who was notorious for dealing out savage bites to his handlers if they made a false move. The first we knew of the assassination attempt was the thumping of little hooves against the wooden sides of his stable, and the shrieks of pain from the three would-be hit-men trapped inside. The net result was that Bruneval remained undamaged whilst two of the killers suffered broken ribs and the third had a broken nose and concussion.

Not every senior NCO in the Parachute Regiment in 1960 fitted the stereotype of ruthless efficiency that the Paras have since acquired from Northern Ireland and the

Falklands. My platoon sergeant in A Company was eccentric, to say the least. He was a little Irishman with an unusual way of going about his business. We were moving out on exercise for a fairly long period so all bedding had to be handed in to the company stores. Our sergeant was Acting Company Quartermaster Sergeant, and he was determined to create a good impression in the hope that he might make the promotion permanent.

It was Friday and we were moving out on Monday morning at about 0930. Because most people left camp over the weekend, he wanted us all to hand in our bedding before we dispersed. But not everyone was going away, of course, so he then decided that we could keep our mattresses, hand the other bedding in, and use our sleeping-bags. Meanwhile, he decided to put a notice into the company routine orders that he wanted all outstanding mattresses returned to the store by 0800 on Monday morning. Unfortunately, while he was writing the orders, the company commander phoned him to discuss some other stores matters and when he got down to finishing them, the mattress problem had gone clean out of his thoughts.

Monday morning arrived and our sergeant is running about organizing stores, rations, weapons and all the other details that come up on a big move. Suddenly he realizes that he's forgotten to ask for the mattresses back. Bugger! But there's no time to type up a notice now, nobody will spot it, and, anyway, he's not entirely sure how to spell mattress, and doesn't want to look like an idiot in front of the company commander. Instead, he uses his 'airborne initiative' and come about 0700 hours he runs down to the stores, gets a hammer and a six-inch nail, nails a six-foot mattress to the notice board, and writes on it in blue chalk 'These will be handed in by 0800 this morning'.

He had no sense of proportion whatsoever, and you only had to make the slightest mistake to get extra guards and duties which he would never rescind. I'd managed to fall foul of him one day for no particularly good reason and collected three extra guard duties as a result. Pissed off by this and with nothing to lose I was determined to get my revenge on him. As it happened, we were doing a parachute jump that day, and our sergeant incautiously asked me to sort out his container for him and get it loaded on the aircraft, as he hadn't time to do it himself. No problem. Once I'd got my hands on his container, it was easy enough to acquire a two-hundredweight block of concrete of the right size, load that in, and then to bend back the retaining pin so that he couldn't easily open it.

We fitted our 'chutes, got in the aircraft and took off, heading for the DZ (drop zone) at Ladies Mile Beach. As the jump approached, we got up to sort out our equipment and it was then that our sergeant noticed something was wrong. Realizing that his container weighed at least twice what it should have done, he demanded, 'What the hell have you done, Scholey?'

By now the red light was on and we were hooked on, ready to jump. The doors were opened, the green light came on and out we went. Although our sergeant was only just ahead of me in the stick, he hit the ground some time before me, probably towed in by the weight of his container.

'Scholey, you bastard! You're on guard tonight!'

'You've already put me on guard tonight, Sergeant.'

Even better, because he couldn't undo the container, the silly sod actually picked it up and carried it on his shoulder the two miles to the RV (rendezvous), rather than simply leaving it where it was.

As a trained driver, I was given quite a lot of driving

details soon after I joined the battalion, ranging from transporting the company to the Troodos mountains for training to moving equipment to various locations around the island. On one occasion I was detailed to go to Nicosia in a 3-ton Bedford R.L. to collect a horse which the battalion had acquired for adventurous training purposes.

I got the horse, which was called Brandy, onto the back of the truck and the vet, who was accompanying it, helped me secure it to the frame that normally held the canopy. The weather was hot, so when we set off, the horse was actually enjoying the cool breeze of the vehicle, which was travelling at a reasonable speed.

Nowadays Cyprus is a very modern and sophisticated place with motorways and dual carriageways crisscrossing the Greek side of the island, but at that time most of the roads were little more than dirt tracks. About halfway back to Limassol, we suddenly came face to face with three large, black American-style Fords travelling at high speed. The track was pretty narrow and there was nowhere for me to go so I brought the truck to a halt, but the driver of the leading Ford decided to try to sweep round me. He didn't make it. As the two cars behind screeched to a halt, the front one slid some twenty metres down the embankment at the side of the road. Fortunately it didn't roll, and the passengers all got out, shaken but uninjured.

While the vet kept Brandy calm I went over to the Cypriots and offered them a hand. After a little pushing and pulling, we managed to haul the car back onto the road using my truck's winch, at a place where all three cars could get past. I hadn't taken much notice of the passengers who'd got out of the car but as they were about to set off, one of them walked over to me, shook my hand and said: *'Endaxi, endaxi.*'

* Thank you, thank you.

And I found myself looking at Archbishop Makarios who had just become the President of Cyprus.

Being in Cyprus also allowed me to get to work on my piss-up technique. The great joy of overseas service in the British army has always been the widespread availability of alcohol at kamikaze prices and warm weather is always conducive to a bit of a drink-up. Although the emergency in Cyprus had ended, it was still not advisable to go out of camp in groups of less than four, so Jock Thompson, Brummie Hassall, Lippy Lipton and I went down to Limassol together for a big night on the Bacardi and Cokes. Around about 2 o'clock in the morning, Jock and I found ourselves on our own, so we decided to get a taxi back to camp. Being half cut we poured ourselves into a grotty and dilapidated Greek-Cypriot taxi. After about fifteen minutes going through the back streets of Limassol – and in those days it was somewhat less charming than it is now – Jock and I began to get suspicious, imagining we were being Shanghaied to a hideous death at the hands of EOKA.

The driver claimed not to speak a word of English, and as we got more agitated, we began a big argument with him in sign language and loud shouts, but no matter what we said and mimed, he would not stop to let us out. By now we had convinced ourselves that we were in for a duffing up at the very least and were desperate to escape.

Then Jock had a brainwave. As a good Scot, he often wore a kilt when out and about, and he happened to have it on that night. He stood up as close to the driver as he could in the back of a cab and dropped his kilt over the poor man's head. The driver let out a muffled scream and slammed on the brakes, the car skidded round then rolled slowly onto its side.

We got out, uninjured, and as we ran from the irate Cypriot, Jock shouted back, 'Just remember, matey, it's Arabs and Scots that wear skirts. The difference is that Arabs wear underpants as well!'

As we turned the corner, the poor taxi driver was still spitting bits of unidentified fluff from his mouth.

Jock Thompson could be something of a monster. At one point he had just received his Post Office savings book back from the UK where he had sent it to get it updated and decided to treat himself to a big night out in Heroes Square in Limassol.

Around five the next morning he arrived back at camp looking completely poleaxed, complaining that he'd been rolled by some bird in a brothel who'd pinched the best part of his two hundred notes. By Naafi break at ten, he had sobered up a bit and was seething with righteous indignation at being the victim of a heinous crime, even though, by all accounts, he'd got pissed and spent most of the money buying drinks for the girls at the bar. Nevertheless, he was not going to let it pass and after work he got another two hundred quid from the Post Office and recruited a couple of mates to go with him to smash up the brothel on the promise of free drinks. They got dressed up in their jeans and bovver boots, and off downtown they went.

Nothing was heard of the punitive raid until the next morning, when a taxi pulled up outside the main gates of the camp and out poured Jock and his two mates. When we enquired whether they had done the place over, the response was: 'No. After drinking ten pints Jock fell in love with one of the girls and blew another £200.'

But all play and no work makes Paras dull boys and in 1961 my first operational deployment duly came along.

On 19 June 1961, a new treaty came into force under

which the government of the oil-rich statelet of Kuwait assumed full responsibility for its foreign affairs, after many years in which the British Empire had effectively controlled it, without ever having full legal responsibility. On 25 June 1961, the Iraqi government, under the dictator General Qasim, announced its intention to annexe Kuwait and began massing troops on the border. Sounds familiar? I thought so.

In fact, the new treaty specified that Britain would continue to be responsible for the defence of Kuwait and the nearest available unit able to get out to the Gulf and put in a block was 2 Para from Cyprus.

The original plan was for a para drop but the winds were too fierce and instead we flew by British Eagle Airways from RAF Akrotiri to Kuwait and were then bussed to the Mutla Ridge, north of Kuwait city, to await whichever came first: British reinforcements or Iraqi invasion.

On the ridge itself, the ground was too rocky to dig in so we moved back to the reverse slope, leaving pickets out to give us advance warning of any Iraqi move, and then we waited.

Now I don't want to sound like a smart-arse, but when I read *Bravo Two-Zero* and the other books about the Gulf War, and saw the lads' descriptions of how they'd been screwed by the weather, I thought to myself: they should have asked me! Because, much to my surprise, even though it was steaming hot during the day it got bloody freezing cold at night, and this was in July. We were lucky enough to have quite a few Second World War veterans in the battalion, and they knew enough about desert conditions to ensure that we were issued with big greatcoats you could snuggle up in after the sun went down.

We'd been there on our own for a couple of days when the Commando carrier – in fact a converted aircraft carrier –

HMS *Bulwark* arrived, carrying with it 42 Commando, Royal Marines.

If the Parachute Regiment is the finest airborne infantry in the world – and it is – the Royal Marines are the best amphibious soldiers. This was the first time I'd really come across them, and I have to say I was impressed. They were smart, fit, keen and skilled, just like us. What's more, although I didn't know it then, they included amongst their number a certain Second Lieutenant Paddy Ashdown, serving as a troop commander: one of those all too rare politicians with operational military service.

So there we were: a battalion of Marines on the right flank, a battalion of Paras on the left, and assorted support elements dragged in from Kenya, Cyprus and Aden to our rear. On paper, not much of a force to hold off the Iraqi army with their tanks and air support. But the paper equation isn't always accurate. The reality was that we were itching for them to come over, because we would have given them a hell of a thumping.

With the arrival of the Marines, A Company was pushed forward about ten miles as a screen, sitting on the Kuwait to Basra road whilst the diplomats and politicians played chicken with each other.

After a couple of months, we were relieved in the line by 3 Para, our sister battalion, who were then based in Bahrain, and in fact we continued to swap with them until the crisis came to an end when the Iraqis backed down in October. With that, we returned to Cyprus, the Marines went wherever Marines go, and General Qasim was brutally murdered by other members of his government.

Back in Cyprus we returned to the usual round of training and duties. Two or three times every week we would go parachuting before breakfast at the DZ on the salt flats next to Ladies Mile Beach, between Akrotiri and Episkopi, and we would regularly visit the training area at Akamus in the west of the island for field training exercises, often against a live enemy.

On one such exercise, our enemy was the Black Watch, the famous Scottish infantry battalion. About midnight one night, I was part of a patrol that went out to recce the Jock position. We came back, reported the info and were then sent out in platoon strength as a fighting patrol to attack them. We hit their position, there was a bit of a kick up, they gave us a bit of a bashing, but all in all we got out okay.

So now they decided they must send a fighting patrol against us. We had met some of them on a social occasion, so we knew that they had a big rugby player, a kind of man-mountain known as 'Big Angus'. They sent out their patrol, but we managed to ambush it and duffed them up. In the dark, we heard the order go down the line: 'Get Big Angus. Get Big Angus, he'll sort them out.'

A couple of hours later, they came back and we ambushed them again. There was much firing of blanks and thunder-flash flares lit up the sky. Then it went quiet until a little Scottish voice called: 'Get a stretcher. The Paras have clobbered Big Angus!'

After six more months in Cyprus, the battalion returned to the UK, taking up temporary residence in Guillemont Barracks, at Cove near Aldershot, before returning to the Middle East to relieve 3 Para as the garrison in Bahrain. We also lost our very popular CO, Lieutenant Colonel Frank King (who went on to become General Sir Frank King), and this was accompanied by a perceptible rise in the bullshit level as the battalion got into the round of parades, duties and demonstrations that accompanied the Bahrain posting.

By mid 1962, I'd regained my second stripe and I was still enjoying myself, but I had begun to look around for something else to do in order to maintain my motivation and enthusiasm for the job.

In the early 1960s, the SAS wasn't the super-glamorous organization that it has since become – in the eyes of the rest of the army, that is. In fact, at that time, 22 SAS was very small – just two under-strength operational squadrons – run on a shoestring and very poorly paid because you had to give up your previous rank when you joined. Nevertheless, I'd heard enough about it to know that the selection course was a challenge I wanted to attempt, and after chatting it through with a few of the lads, I began to work on my fitness with a view to doing selection when we got back to the UK.

After a year in Bahrain we came home and settled back into life at Guillemont Barracks. Bullshit and discipline were, if anything, even more strictly enforced than in Bahrain and if we weren't out on exercise, we were back in the block polishing the soles of our spare pair of gym shoes, or some equally fascinating task. To make sure that we did actually 'screw the nut', we were always being inspected by somebody or other, ranging from our platoon sergeant up to the commanding officer and, of course, everything had to be pretty well immaculate.

On one weekly inspection, our company sergeant major was carrying out a pre-inspection to make sure that everything was okay prior to the arrival of the CO and the RSM. We were standing by our beds, rigidly to attention, as the CSM cruised through the billet, checking this and that, making sure that everything was spick and span.

Having completed one side of the room, we seemed to be doing well, with only two men charged: one for dirty boots, one for long hair. By now he had reached my mate John

Wriles and went to his big green metal locker, standing as they do in uniform line against the wall. Everything looked in good order so far, but when he eased the locker out from the wall to see if it had been dusted at the back, a big black spider ran across the back of his locker and scuttled inside. The sergeant major put him on a charge and he was given seven days confined to Barracks.

When he returned, looking glum-faced and miserable, we asked him what he had been charged with.

'Keeping a pet without authority.'

No question, the army has always had a strange sense of fun. When I eventually put in my request to be allowed to do SAS selection, I found myself waiting outside the CO's office with an old corporal called Fergie. Now, Fergie had been in the army commandos during the war and had a distinguished record, but latterly he had been working in the officers' mess as a steward. Now he was approaching his last six months in the army and had decided that he wanted to serve it out as a proper soldier in a rifle company.

As Fergie and I stood outside the CO's office, the drill sergeant came up and asked, 'Corporals Ferguson and Scholey . . . what do youse two want?'

We explained and he laughed.

'SAS selection, you must be fucking joking! And, Fergie, you're on a charge: you're improperly dressed.'

'What do you mean, improperly dressed? This is my best uniform.'

'You haven't got your false teeth in.'

'Look, sir, I want to talk to the Colonel, not eat him.'

I burst out laughing and we both got three days jankers (confined to barracks). Thanks for that.

CHAPTER THREE

There were three of us from 2 Para going up to Hereford for our shot at SAS selection in August 1963: me, Brummie Hassall and Alan Lonney. We'd all been training hard and I was certainly as fit as I'd ever been in my life, but what was bothering me was the uncertainty and mystery that surrounded the whole process. In the battalion we had a couple of lads who'd done a tour with the SAS and come back, and a good handful who'd failed selection at one time or another, so we'd been pumping them for information and we knew that we were in for a rough few weeks as we were beasted about the Welsh countryside.

But what was less clear was what the SAS was looking for apart from physical fitness – and everyone I'd spoken to reckoned that fitness on its own wasn't enough. From what I'd heard, the SAS looked for a certain 'X-factor' in its soldiers: a combination of intelligence, initiative and imagination, and if you didn't have it you might as well not turn up. Having acquired a reputation in the battalion as a bit of a clown, everyone I'd spoken to was convinced I didn't have *it*. Word on the street was: 'SAS selection? Scholey's got no fucking chance.' But I thought they were wrong.

Just before we left, we got a little chat from Drum Major Williams. He told me, 'Corporal Scholey, tomorrow you're going from the 2nd Battalion of the Parachute Regiment – the finest regiment in the British Army – to the Special Air Service, another fine regiment. I don't want to see you back here unless you've earned the beret and badge that they wear.' He didn't have to say that – what did he care about the SAS? – but I was determined not to let him down. So I continued to clown around as usual, but underneath there was a bit of steel: I wasn't going to fail!

Still, you do have to be fit and Brummie and I had taken some leave to do hill training out in Wales. We booked ourselves accommodation at the training camp at Dering Lines in Brecon, which is handy for the Beacons, and headed on up for ten days' hard work. Unfortunately, we'd had an even harder time from one of the camp staff, a sergeant major with an attitude problem who wanted to pick on us, so eventually we'd decided to stay out in the hills the whole time, bivvying at night in one of the forestry blocks.

On our first morning in Brecon, Brummie and I had gone to the toilets, where they had a set of scales, to weigh our Bergens. I'd packed mine to about thirty-five pounds, which was about the weight we carried in Para training, but Brummie immediately told me, 'No, mate, that's not enough.'

I was a bit surprised by this, because thirty-five pounds was heavy enough for me.

'What do you mean? How much do they want?' I asked.

'You've got to have fifty-five pounds in your pack, and don't forget you're carrying a rifle as well. That's another fourteen . . .'

'That's bollocks, Brummie, nobody can carry that much . . .' But he was right, and we spent the next ten days humping these huge rucksacks over the hills, marching from point to point as we tried to accustom ourselves to the monstrous loads and tricky terrain.

So as we arrived at Hereford on that summer afternoon, and we unloaded our kit-bags and suitcases onto platform two, I would have to admit that I was more than a little anxious about what was going to happen next, and from the looks on their faces, I could tell that the same was true for the others as well. As we walked out of the station into the car park, the first thing to confront us was a green Bedford 3-ton truck with a small blue square painted with the winged-dagger badge on the bonnet: our transport into Bradbury Lines.

Brummie walked over to see whether the driver was in it and came back to report that there was nobody about but the keys were in the ignition. This started an immediate debate: was it an initiative test? Were we already being observed to see how we would react to this unexpected situation? There were a few other squaddies from different units who had been on the same train as us and they came over to join in the argument. The question was this: should we wait for a driver to appear to take us to the camp, should we ignore the truck and make our own way there, or should we take the truck and drive ourselves there? We were still arguing over this a couple of minutes later when I heard a friendly voice behind us: 'All right, lads? Sorry I'm late, chuck your kit in the back and climb aboard . . .'

I turned round to see a scruffy-looking ginger-haired soldier wearing a sandy-coloured beret with a cloth winged-dagger badge, a faded camouflaged windproof smock with a hood, and a *Daily Mirror* tucked under his arm. 'I've just been over the road for a cup of tea and I didn't hear the train come in.'

We piled in the back and as the truck started up, Brummie leaned over and nudged me: 'That was lucky.'

This was the first time that I had been to Hereford (you

might say I've never really left it since) and on the short drive through I was able to see what a lovely little town it is. The main features are the river Wye, which winds through the middle, and the cathedral, which sits just on the edge of the town centre. In those days, before developers began to get their hands on it, most of the buildings were old and original, and the whole place had a kind of unspoiled charm that you don't really see nowadays.

Bradbury Lines was a Second World War wooden-hutted camp on the outskirts of the town, just beginning to get a bit shabby, but ideally suited for a small regiment that didn't have a lot of vehicles or heavy kit, and did most of its training elsewhere. It had the usual fixtures and fittings of an army camp: a parade square, drill sheds and neatly tended flower beds, but there was something odd about it as well, and it took me a while to realize what it was. Unlike every other army base I'd ever been on – and having been a truckie, a Gunner and a Para, I'd been on a few by now – it was quiet.

Now I don't mean that it was silent like a monastery or anything daft like that, but there was nobody shouting or yelling at us, nobody doing drill, nobody doubling about. There was an air of quiet professionalism if you like – completely unlike the usual noise, bustle and bullshit of a regular army unit. Mind you, a big part of the reason was simply numbers: in 1963 the Regiment only had two squadrons, and they were on operations most of the time, so there was hardly anyone there!

When we arrived, we were taken down to Selection Troop to book in. As I waited in the corridor outside the office, I had a chance to look at the various notices stuck to the wall. Alongside the standard military-issue training posters were a lot of photographs of SAS soldiers on operations and training in various exotic locations, and some framed proverbs and sayings. I'd seen or heard most of them before, but they weren't the sort of thing you normally found pinned on the walls in regimental training wings:

Many are called, few are chosen.
A Guerilla is a Fish that Swims in a Friendly Sea.
Recruit to Sergeant: 'Sergeant, if I don't classify on the range, will it stop me going abroad?'
Sergeant: 'No, son, but it's likely to stop you coming back.'

Pretty corny, but different. The other surprise was that the whole permanent selection set up consisted of a captain, a squadron quartermaster sergeant and a clerk. There were other instructors, of course, but they were busy doing other things, and not hanging around waiting to give us a hard time, which is what would have happened in the rest of the army. Instead, the captain told us that we had to parade the next morning at 0800 hours and sent us down to the stores to collect our kit.

Now, I had half an idea that we would end up with armfuls of specialist kit, which would fit in with the slightly mysterious reputation that the SAS had, but I was soon put right. We got a bolt-action Lee-Enfield No. 4 rifle with no sling, a dog-eared old Bergen rucksack, a prismatic compass, a couple of maps, a belt and a pair of water-bottles, and that was it. No x-ray spectacles, no exploding cigars, no James Bond kit at all. Oh, well, that'll come later, I thought.

The accommodation was pretty basic – a bed and a locker in a twelve-man room in a wooden hut – so getting settled in didn't take too long, and then Alan, Brummie and I wandered off down town for a pint and some fish and chips to prepare for the action tomorrow.

The whole selection course was at muster parade at 0800 hours. Alongside the three of us from 2 Para there were a few more from other battalions of the Parachute Regiment, a handful from other parts of 16 Para Brigade, distinctive in their maroon berets, and a great mass from all parts of the army, not to mention the Marines, RAF, RAF Regiment and the Navy, coming to 130 candidates in all. The instructors called the roll and came up one short: 'Edwards? Where's Edwards?'

A voice answered up: 'He was late into breakfast, Staff, he's on his way.'

A couple of minutes passed and then Edwards trotted up and reported to the instructor. 'Sorry I'm late, Staff, permission to fall in?'

'Just go in the office a second, will you, they've got something for you.'

They did: a rail warrant back to his unit. He hadn't even made it to the first event. These guys were serious. After this, we got a quick pep talk from Captain Wilson, then it was onto the trucks and off up to Dinedor Hill, which overlooks Hereford, for lessons in map reading.

No question, after the dismissal of Edwards the first day of selection was a bit of an anticlimax. We sat on top of Dinedor with our maps and compasses as the Training Wing staff ensured that everybody there had sufficient navigating ability to get through the early part of the course. Map reading shouldn't have been too much of a problem for us infantry soldiers, of course, but the idea was to make sure that nobody would suffer just because their military background didn't require them to have certain skills. In any case, there was still a feeling in the army at that time that maps and map reading were for officers, and I can't say I was completely familiar with all the precepts. This was followed in the afternoon by a couple of lectures in first aid and basic survival, and then we knocked off, in good time for me, Alan and Brummie to get down for more beer and fish and chips after first getting our kit together and having the evening meal in the cookhouse.

The second day was when the fun started. The main activity, after we'd mustered at 0800, was to get on the trucks for a short drive out to the Malvern Hills, twenty miles or so to the east of Hereford. Once we'd disembarked and formed up in threes, we were detailed off with our instructors and sent off on a fourteen-mile speed march over the hills, carrying our rifles and Bergens weighted at 55 pounds (thanks, Brummie!).

Well, not too difficult, apart from the weight, but this was when reality hit home for the lads who hadn't prepared themselves properly, and it wasn't long before people started dropping out. It was seven miles out, a quick stop for a rest and a brew, then seven back; but as we formed up in threes at this big car park – called 'British Camp' – a little sickener was thrown in by Captain Wilson.

'Right, lads, well done. Now I want you to take five minutes to grab a breather and sort your kit out, then we'll be running back to Hereford.'

For the first split second after this announcement, I nearly fainted. Bloody hell! Hereford was twenty miles away, I was carrying fifty-five pounds on my back, and I was shagged out after doing fourteen hard miles on the Malverns. But then reality kicked in. Brummie was next to me, and as we bent down, taking swigs from our water-bottles, tightening straps on our belt order and Bergens, and getting ourselves sorted, I said to him, 'Don't worry, mate, it's a con.'

'What do you mean?'

'There's no way they're going to run us all the way back to Hereford. Look at them. They've all been on operations till a couple of weeks back, they're married with families waiting for them, and they've got to take us out again tomorrow. If they run back with us, they'll be completely fucked as well. I reckon they've got the trucks parked up a couple of miles down the road.'

Brummie took a look at the rest of the course, half of them dressed in weird and wonderful 'magic' gear.

'Scholey, you're right. They're just getting rid of the Walter Mittys.'

We'd just got ourselves sorted out when the order came from one of the Training Wing staff sergeants: 'Course! Course, 'shun!'

We braced up into the position of attention.

'Course will move to the left in threes. Left TURN!'

We dutifully obliged.

'By the right, double MARCH!'

And off we set. By now, the murmurs of disquiet at the idea of running back to Hereford were growing, and it wasn't long before the first few lads started to drop out with 'muscle strains' and 'twisted ankles'.

Well, fair enough, but on SAS selection there are no second chances, and anyone who jacked now was off the course for good. Sure enough, we jogged on down the road for a mile or so, rounded a corner and there were the trucks, lined up to take us back to camp. We'd lost about fifteen off the course already.

It's always been the same on selection courses. A lot of the people there have come for the wrong reasons: they're bored with conventional soldiering; they've spent too long in Germany; they don't get on with the other guys in their units; they're looking for a change. There's nothing wrong with that, but if you don't have sufficient motivation, you simply won't pass. It's too hard.

But you also get the Walter Mittys. These are the guys who turn up with all the extra kit: special foods; go-faster boots;

weird and wonderful combat kit, and so on. There's nothing particularly wrong with that, if the gear is useful, but the point about selection is that you don't need it. If you can do the course comfortably in the clothing and equipment you've been issued, then why bother bringing all the other stuff? Wearing flash kit won't help you get over the hills any quicker, but it will attract the attention of the training staff, and that's the last thing you want. A good example of this happened a few years ago.

A young parachute-trained officer was going through the special officers'-week section of the course, part of which involves standing in front of an audience of experienced SAS officers, NCOs and troopers to give presentations and talks, under hostile questioning. As it happened, this officer was wearing a set of jungle combats onto which he had sewn his British Parachute wings, as per regulations, on his right sleeve, and a set of American Para wings on his left breast above his pocket. Now this is quite a common practice in the airborne brigade, but in the SAS, where you rarely see anybody wearing badges other than on their beret, it attracts attention. One of the questions the young officer was inevitably asked was, 'Why have you sewn American Para wings on your shirt? Are you trying to impress us?' Well, there's no answer to that, and of course the extra stress certainly didn't help him. This was compounded the next day because he removed the wings and was inevitably asked, 'Why have you taken those American Para wings off? Do you always do what NCOs tell you?'

The moral of this tale is that once you get noticed, you can't win. Of course, officers' week is something I've never been through – thank God! It's a constant moan with some of my old mates that nearly all the officers we have in the Regiment are rubbish, but I think they're wrong. You do get some rotten apples, of course, but by and large they're good soldiers who are keen to learn, and when they've spent a few years in the Regiment, they often end up making a bigger contribution than some of the non-commissioned ranks who've been in much longer. And anyone who's been through officers' week successfully has my respect!

In the seventies, a retired member of the Regiment, known as 'Drag', was employed as range warden for the SAS training areas. Although he was in his late fifties, Drag was a keen marathon runner long before it became a mass-participation sport and was super-fit, as well as possessing a wicked, dry sense of humour.

During one officers' week, when Lofty Wiseman was the Training Wing sergeant major, all the hopeful young Ruperts had been at a lecture given by the second in command which was supposed to be followed by 'fitness training'. Lofty had the officers standing outside Training Wing as he called the roll when Drag happened to walk past, carrying a couple of shredded targets off to the target shed to be repaired.

Now Drag was dressed in a donkey jacket, a threadbare checked shirt, old corduroys held up with baler twine and grotty wellies, and combined with his bald head and grubbiness (he had just been cleaning up the pistol range), he looked every inch the village idiot, rather than the experienced, if retired, SAS veteran he actually was. This gave Lofty, who was supposed to be leading the officers on a road run, an idea.

'Mr Rowbottom! Wait a moment, I've got a job for you.'

Somehow, Drag sensed that a gag was coming up and played along, tugging at his forelock. 'Yes, Mr Wiseman, sir!'

'I'm a bit busy at the moment. Would you mind taking these gentlemen for a run?'

'Right-oh, sir!'

Drag dropped the two targets on the verge outside training wing, and carefully laid his donkey jacket on top of them. Standing in front of the squad of officers in cords and wellies: 'Right, gents, left turn, by the front, double march . . .'

And off they went, a scruffy civilian leading a squad of bewildered officers. An hour and a half later they returned, Drag still leading despite his wellies. The only one of the officers to stay with him slumped on the grass in disbelief.

'That little bastard just took us on a twelve-mile run!'

I suspect the best advice I could give to anyone attempting selection is this: expect the unexpected!

After the first run on my selection, we got back to camp and were paraded outside Training Wing. Captain Wilson stood in front of us.

'Okay, gentlemen, that was an easy introduction. From now on, the marches get longer, harder and faster.'

He wasn't joking.

The next three weeks were hard work. Every morning we would parade at the crack of sparrowfart, with our Bergens, webbing and rifle, and pile onto the three-tonners for the drive to the Beacons. As we got close to the mountains, the trucks would separate and eventually they would begin dropping us off, one at a time. We were called out of the back, given the grid reference where we were, the grid reference for the place we had to get to, and that was it, the truck would bugger off. Even so, you couldn't just stand there in the road looking at your map, you had to stay switched on and semi-tactical. This meant that as soon as we got our instructions, we had to scuttle into the hedge to start working out the navigation, and then get moving quickly.

The first march was ten or twelve miles and there were about five truckloads of recruits, but as the distances lengthened, the course thinned out so that by the end there was just

one truckload when we began the final endurance march: and
this the monster!

But even before the endurance march, I'd had my own
frightener. Out on the Beacons, I made a stupid mistake. I
wasn't too confident in my map reading at the time, and I
decided to follow a bunch of soldiers who were walking down
a ridgeline about half a mile ahead of me. Trouble was, when
I got close I realized that they were from the battle school at
Brecon: nothing to do with the SAS at all! Cobblers! By then
I was miles out of my way, and I knew I wasn't going to make
it to the last RV in time. Still, I wasn't about to give up. I
eventually got there, in pouring rain, at about one in the
morning and discovered, with no great surprise, that there
was nobody about. I found a phone box and called in.
Whoever was on duty made me describe my surroundings, so
he could be sure I'd actually got there, then told me to make
my way back to the small training camp that was serving as
our base.

I got there two hours later, wet, cold and shattered. The
instructor on duty in the office showed me into a large room,
littered with wet, snoring bodies: 'Get your head down in
there, son.'

I took off my boots and smock, unrolled my sleeping bag
and lay down. It seemed as if I'd blinked, then it was morning. An hour or so later, we were parading for the next march
and the Training Wing sergeant major asked, 'Where's the
lad who came in at three in the morning?'

'Sir.' I put my hand up.

'You'll want to drop out, then, I expect.' It almost sounded
like an instruction.

'No, thank you, sir. I'd like to carry on.'

'Okay, that's fine.' It was a lucky escape. If I hadn't made it
to the last RV, they would have binned me from the course.

Not surprisingly, the final march was the longest of the course and covered all of forty-five miles through six RV points, starting at the Talybont reservoir and heading out over the top of Pen-y-Fan, past the Storey Arms, over the Black Mountain and back, starting at 0830 on the Thursday morning, and finishing before 1230 on Friday. No easy task at any time, but by this stage, three weeks of humping over the mountains with a heavy rucksack had taken its toll on all of us. We all had little injuries like blisters and Bergen burns, and some of the lads were carrying more serious problems that they'd picked up out on the hills: twisted ankles and knees, bruises, sprains, the whole lot.

Having said that, the weather conditions were fair and I made good time after we set off, getting through the first four checkpoints before nightfall. Not that anyone told me I was doing well or anything nice like that! When you got to the RVs they simply checked that you were physically all right then gave you the grid reference for the next RV. Thanks, lads. Still, I have to admit it was a system I got to quite like: a good soldier – a good anything, come to that – shouldn't need someone to tell him how clever he is every time he does something well.

By the time I got to the last leg, every bone and muscle in my body was aching. At 1000 I reached the last RV, back at the reservoir, and checked in. Nobody said much, except that we couldn't go back to camp until everyone was in, so I walked off a little way, took off my Bergen and settled down to make a brew. It was the strangest sensation: taking off the Bergen was like putting on a jet-pack: I thought I was going to lift off at any moment and float away. Once I'd brewed up, I sat down with my back resting against it to drink my tea and wait for the others. I tell you, my eyelids ached I was so tired.

But it wasn't really till the next day that the pain hit home. By then even my aches were aching, and although we'd been debriefed and I'd found out – along with Brummie and Alan – that I was one of the nine who'd passed (out of 130), all I could think of was getting my head down for some rest before the next phase of the course started.

Well, that wasn't too far off. Next step was jungle training out in Borneo, and for this we were marrying up with the previous course who'd been doing their continuation training in and around the camp. The reason for this was simple: with only two squadrons, both of which were committed to operational theatres, there weren't enough experienced instructors around to run separate jungle courses, and there were so few people getting through selection that it wasn't economic to set up a whole jungle course for a handful of students.

I enjoyed my first experience of the jungle, and I enjoyed working with the instructors, who were incredibly professional. If you'd asked most civilians at that time what the SAS was, the few who could have given you an answer would probably have told you about David Stirling and desert operations in the Second World War, but the real home of the SAS, at that time anyway, was the jungle.

Back in the late 1940s, Communist guerrillas in Malaya, who had fought against the Japanese with our help during the Second World War, had decided to turn on us, even though we were in the process of handing over the government of Malaya to the Malays. The Communists had then started a terrorist and guerrilla campaign, basing themselves in the jungle, which they could use as a safe haven, and coming out to strike at military and civilian targets, more or less at will. Britain and the rest of the Commonwealth decided to resist this and sent in the army.

But there were problems: the British Army's main task

then was in Europe and most of the training was geared towards that; and British Army units themselves had a large proportion of National Service soldiers and officers who lacked the experience and know-how you need for internal security and counter-insurgency tasks in the jungle environment. The upshot of this was that, although things improved in some parts of Malaya, the security forces lost control of the jungle to the guerrillas.

The man who was brought in to sort the situation out was a Second World War veteran called Mike Calvert. He had been one of the earliest volunteers for the Commandos when they were formed in 1940, and had gone on to serve in the Chindits in Burma and at the very end of the war he became commander of the SAS Brigade, which was then made up of two British regiments, 1 and 2 SAS, two French regiments (the 1st and 2nd RCP), and a Belgian squadron, together with various attached arms and whatnot. After the war Calvert, like most regular soldiers, had had to drop down in rank to carry on in the forces, in his case from brigadier down to major, but he'd soldiered on as a staff officer until the call came to go out to Malaya.

Calvert spent about six months studying the problem then sat down to write a report that covered most of the major faults in the campaign so far. The biggest problem was caused by bickering and in-fighting amongst the high command, but he also identified a need to take the war into the jungle, and to get the jungle people on our side so that they wouldn't provide support for the guerrillas. He also reckoned that a special unit should be formed for deep patrolling and 'hearts and minds' operations and, after his report had been accepted, he was handed the job of raising and training the unit, which was given the name 'The Malayan Scouts'.

The Malayan Scouts had a bumpy start, but after a couple of years' hard work it began to be a real success, not only in running its own operations, but in showing the rest of the army in Malaya that they could stay in the jungle for much longer than they imagined possible. It wasn't too long before the unit was made a permanent part of the army as 22 SAS Regiment. At that time, there were three British SAS squadrons: A, B and D; a Rhodesian squadron, C; a New Zealand SAS squadron; and a squadron of volunteers from the Parachute Regiment.

So, in 1963 when I turned up, almost all the instructors were Malaya veterans, while some of them had been in Korea and a few had seen service in the Second World War (one lad, Bert Perkins in D Squadron, had been at the Anzio landings in 1943, fought with the Glosters at the battle of the Imjin river in 1951, spent two years as a prisoner of the Chinese and joined the Regiment almost as soon as he got back!). If these guys told you something, you listened, because they had been there, seen it and done it: they knew what worked and what didn't; and they knew when one of their students was bluffing.

The first part of the jungle training was pretty basic. We learned the rudiments of living in the jungle: putting up A-frame shelters; first aid; survival techniques, and so on. From there we moved on to the basics of patrolling: movement which left as little sign as possible; navigation in an environment where you can rarely see good landmarks; maintaining good communications. Then it was tactics: contact drills; ambush drills; anti-ambush drills; close target reconnaissance; all done thoroughly, efficiently and using live ammunition. Finally, we began to put it all together in a series of exercises under the watchful eyes of the instructors, working together as a team.

Of course, the main purpose of the jungle training was just that, teaching us jungle warfare, but not far behind came the selection aspect as well. To succeed in the SAS, where you're often working alone or in very small groups, you need to be an individualist, but you also have to be able to fit in with a team and work well together for extended periods. If you're so horrible that the rest of the patrol want to kill you after two days of operations, you're actually going to be an impediment, and there's no better place to find out who doesn't fit in than the jungle, where everyday life puts you under more than enough pressure.

With the jungle course finished, it was back to Hereford for continuation training in the skills required for an SAS soldier. Apart from the obvious ones – advanced weapons training in Nato and foreign weaponry, communications with various sorts of radio, sabotage and demolitions, first aid and all the rest of it – we also had language aptitude tests, mortar and artillery control, an introduction to air controlling, combat survival, resistance to interrogation and a range of other subjects that wouldn't necessarily spring to mind as part and parcel of the individual skills a soldier might need.

The end of the training came after the combat survival course. The lads who weren't from airborne units were sent off to Abingdon to do their para course with the RAF and the rest of us paraded in one of the lecture rooms.

At that time, the CO was Lieutenant Colonel John Woodhouse, who'd been with the Regiment more or less since Calvert had reformed it. More than anyone else he was responsible for turning the Regiment into what it later became: he had devised the selection course and insisted on the highest imaginable standards for anyone coming into the Regiment; and he had been at the forefront of developing many of the techniques that we used in operations and training. As an officer and a leader, he had the absolute respect of every man in the Regiment. We were called to attention as the colonel entered. He stood in front of us and smiled.

'Well done, gentlemen. You've passed selection and continuation training, and you have what it takes to begin a career with the SAS. Before you do, there are several things I want you to think about.

'First, no one here is indispensable: you are now beginning a year on probation and if we find you aren't up to the mark after a year, you will be returned to your unit. Having said that, the same will be true throughout the rest of your time with the Regiment.

'Second: rank. If you join the Regiment, you will immediately lose any rank you have and revert to the rank of trooper. You will certainly not be promoted to lance corporal until you can convince us that you are capable of commanding a four man patrol on operations.

'Third: pay. We are an operational regiment. We do not have time to waste pursuing expenses claims and special allowances or queuing at the Pay Office. The only queues I ever want to see will be outside the Operations Room door.

'Fourth: medals. Don't expect medals, you are SAS and much more is expected from you.'

There was no sound. The RSM had a cardboard box containing our sand-coloured SAS berets and parachute wings and he now stepped forward so that the colonel could present them to us. It was one of the proudest moments of my life so far.

So here I was, a probationary member of 22 SAS, all fired up and ready to join D Squadron's Amphibious Troop and to begin the learning process all over again. Since the return to Europe after the Malayan campaign (and the short operation in northern Oman that the Regiment had carried out in 1959), a lot of hard thinking had been carried out.

The upshot of this was a complete reorganization of 22 SAS. The foreign squadrons had been sent home, the Parachute squadron had gone back to the Parachute Regiment and B Squadron had been disbanded and absorbed into A and D Squadrons. The SAS moved back to Britain for the first time, being based in Malvern and then in Hereford.

It had become fairly obvious that the sort of operations the Regiment would be likely to be called upon to carry out needed a much more flexible organization than a regular infantry battalion. In fact, it was decided to abandon regimental level operations and fix deployments at squadron level and below for everything short of all-out war. By the time I joined the Regiment, this had already happened, and although the system had only been running for a year or two, it had proved to be a success and still forms the organizational basis of 22 SAS.

Basing deployment at the squadron level meant that each squadron needed to possess the full range of available talents, so each was established to consist of four sixteen-man troops, with a different specialized 'entry' skill. The four troops were the 'Free Fall' troop, specializing in parachute operations; the 'Rover' troop who would be operating from specially adapted 'Pink Panther' Land Rovers; Amphibious Troop, using canoes and diving techniques; and Mountain Troop.

Within these specializations, each troop had various tasks and standards which had to be achieved in order to give the squadron its required capability, so that, for example, Mountain Troop had to be able to guide a company or squadron-sized unit safely, effectively and tactically on climbs rated at up to 'Very Difficult' standard* and to be able to train a certain number of partisan or irregular troops in mountain warfare; Air Troop were required to be able to parachute from various types of aircraft at high altitude, to mark drop zones and heli-landing sites; and all the myriad special tasks associated with air operations.

My first posting was to D Squadron's Boat Troop, which meant various courses in canoeing, scuba diving and other strange aquatic pastimes. I did these, and hated them, but after a very short period I was shifted to the Rover Troop, 18 Troop, where I was to encounter two big, ugly, complicated things, which were to take on a major significance in my life over the next few years. The first of these was the specially modified, long-range, SAS Pink Panther Land Rover, the second was the Troop Sergeant, Don 'Lofty' Large.

Once you've met Lofty, it's unlikely that you'll ever forget him. Six foot five inches in his socks and built like a brick shithouse, his facial features make him look like Frankenstein's younger brother. But his terrifying appearance was completely deceptive, because Lofty's biggest secret was that he was one of the most laid-back men in the history of the British Army. The reason for this was pretty straightforward. Lofty came from a small village in the Cotswolds, just outside Cheltenham in Gloucestershire, but for some reason he had joined up as a bandsman in the Wiltshires when he was fifteen. Five years later a call came round for volunteers to go to Korea with the Glosters as infantrymen.

Very soon after arriving in Korea, he took part in the battle of the Imjin River when the Glosters were effectively sacrificed to buy time for the rest of the British brigade to

* This is internationally recognized standard of difficulty for climbing.

withdraw in the face of 25,000 or so Chinese soldiers. Lofty had taken two machine-gun bullets in the shoulder and been captured by the Chinese, and along with most of the rest of his battalion, he'd spent the next two years or so in a POW camp, without any real treatment for his wounds and on an inadequate diet that caused him to lose about six stone in weight. Every now and then he was taken out to face pointless, frightening interrogations and, like his comrades he was subjected to continuous propaganda and indoctrination from the Chinese Communists.

Lofty was eventually given early release from the POW camp along with a few others who were judged by the Chinese to be unfit for further military service, and he'd returned to Britain with little prospect of soldiering on. Somehow, through constant effort and determination, he had not only regained his health but got fit enough to take and pass selection for the Regiment. When you've been through a series of experiences like that, you can afford to be pretty relaxed about life!

Lofty had joined D Squadron in Malaya in 1957, gone on to fight with them during the Jebel Akhdar operation and had recently returned to the squadron after spending a couple of years as an instructor with 23 SAS (part of the Territorial Army) in Birmingham.

So it was for Lofty and the other members of the troop to introduce me to one of the Regiment's latest acquisitions: the Pink Panther. The inspiration for these beasties came from the vehicles that had been adapted for use by the Long Range Desert Group and the original SAS during the Second World War. These had been Jeeps and Chevrolet trucks modified with new suspension, special tyres, extra fuel tanks and extra gun-mountings, to give mobility, speed and flexibility to small units working out in the desert. Our version was based on the long wheelbase Land Rover, and carried a huge selection of added equipment and firepower: our personal rifles; two GPMGs on stabilized mountings; an 84mm Carl Gustav anti-tank launcher; front and rear smoke grenade dischargers; a theodolite and sun-compass for desert navigation; a powerful spotlight; different radios for communications with base, ground to air and vehicle to vehicle; sand channels; a motorized winch; cooking equipment; rations; water; extra built-in fuel tanks; patrol kit for dismounted work; in fact, pretty much everything short of the kitchen sink. It always struck me that this was a slightly more civilized way of going about operations than in the other three troop specializations where you were effectively limited – in the field – to the kit you could carry on your back. The only drawback was that the engine was a bit underpowered for all the extra weight that the vehicle was carrying about, and the turning circle was enormous, which made these early Pinkies pretty much useless for operations in North-west Europe. In the desert, though, they were fine.

But the thing everyone noticed about them, and the reason for their name, was the colour we painted them for desert operations: pink. A couple of years later, Lofty and I got sent down to Sandhurst with a Pinkie for some sort of equipment demonstration which was being visited by Field Marshal Montgomery. We'd set up our little stand, with our nicely polished vehicle and various bits and pieces arranged around it, when Monty turned up with his entourage. He must have been well into his seventies by then, but he looked dapper and fit, and he was obviously intrigued by the Land Rover. He walked over to us, and as we saluted said, 'Ah, SAS I see! And who are you?'

'Sergeant Large and Trooper Scholey, sir,' replied Lofty.

'Large, eh? How appwopwiate. Now, tell me, why have you painted this vehicle pink?'

'Well, sir, we have found on operations that this colour actually affords us the best camouflage in the desert. It stems from the Second World War when some tanks had to be put into action before they had been camouflaged. They were painted with a pink-coloured primer, but it seems they were even better camouflaged than vehicles painted a sand colour,' Lofty explained.

'Weally?' said Monty. 'How fascinating. Thank you vewwy much, Sergeant. Cawwy on.' We saluted and Monty moved off, but as he was walking away, he turned to one of his aides and said, in a stage whisper, 'Bollocks!'

Well, I don't know if the story is true or not, but that's what I'd been told as well, and the camouflage certainly did work. On an exercise in the Libyan desert before Colonel Gaddaffi took over the country we were operating against ground and air forces who were trying to locate us. At one stage, we were listening in on the ground-to-air net when we heard a reconnaissance aircraft reporting that he had spotted our position. As he went round for another pass, we moved about 400 metres and that was it. He reported that he'd lost contact and never re-established it: SAS 1; RAF nil.

Apart from getting to grips with the troop vehicles, the other important qualification I needed was my 'patrol skill'. Within each four-man SAS team, it's important that there are a wide range of basic skills, and before you are operationally deployed, you need to qualify in one of them. The key specializations are: communications, demolitions, medic and languages; and, of course, you need a commander as well. Continuation training before you join the squadron gives you a basic grounding in all of them, but I was lucky enough to be selected to do the patrol medic course.

There's a lot of rubbish talked about some aspects of SAS training, and the medic course is one of them. What it doesn't do is turn you into a super surgeon or fully qualified paramedic. The course itself was twelve weeks long, when I did it, and consisted of six weeks in the classroom in Hereford, followed by a six-week attachment in the casualty department of a major hospital, putting the theory of first aid and trauma management into practice under the supervision of qualified doctors and nurses. Together with the first aid, we were being taught how to keep an operational patrol healthy when in the field for extended periods, and a certain amount of general health and hygiene practice that might enable us to assist a doctor or field surgical team if necessary.

Once you qualify as a patrol medic, you have to attend regular refresher training and hospital attachments to keep the qualification, and while this is hard work, it can also be great fun. One time, Taff Springles, a couple of other lads from the squadron and I were doing an attachment at the John Radcliffe Infirmary in Oxford. Taff and I were on shift when a huge, burly man was brought in after falling off a ladder while cleaning his windows. He'd managed to land on his greenhouse, so in addition to his bruises and sprains, he had some nasty lacerations as well. I cleaned and dressed his minor injuries and then, under the supervision of the ward sister, Taff prepared to suture a large cut across his chest. Up until this point, the atmosphere had been light-hearted and jolly but as Taff was getting the gear ready, he asked the sister whether he should use '30' or '50' thread for the stitches. 'Are you sure you're doctors?' our patient asked jokingly. We reassured him and he seemed happy until, after Taff had put a couple of stitches in, he asked the nurse some other question. At this point, the patient narrowed his eyes suspiciously: 'Here, you *are* doctors, aren't you?'

'That's right,' replied Taff.

'Well, if you're doctors, how come you keep having to ask the sister here what to do?'

Taff launched into our prepared cover story. 'Well, we're attached here from a different hospital and we have a different way of working.'

The patient thought about this for a couple of seconds, then jumped up off the trolley: 'Hey, fuck off, man! Listen, I'm a plumber and I can fix pipes in London, Birmingham or Glasgow, 'cos they're all the fucking same!' and with that, he took off through the ward and out into the waiting room, trailing odd bits of swab and bandages behind him. As he passed the other patients in the waiting room, he warned them: 'Hey, you don't want to go in there, they're all fucking amateurs!'

I chased after him and managed to coax him back, so we were able to retrieve the needle and thread from his chest and, eventually, give him the treatment he needed. Later on, at the end of our shift, Taff and I headed down to the local pub for a pie and a pint and who should we see but our patient, drinking with some of his mates. He beckoned us over and bought us a drink and we spent a very pleasant evening with him.

Someone once asked me whether I would be in a position to, say, take out an appendix if a member of my patrol went down with acute appendicitis on an operation and I suppose, yes, in theory I probably could. I certainly knew enough to make a reasonably confident diagnosis of appendicitis; I knew enough anatomy to be able to find it; and enough minor surgical technique to be able to cut it out and close up the incision afterwards. But the fact is that I wouldn't. We also learned that any kind of surgical procedure carried out under operational conditions would be likely to lead to massive infection, whilst my knowledge of surgical technique was not sufficiently comprehensive to deal with any unusual complications, which an experienced surgeon would normally be able to take in his stride. In this – and similar – theoretical circumstances, my response would be to dose the patient with antibiotics until it was possible to evacuate him to trained help. For what it is, the SAS medics course is pretty comprehensive, but basic training for a doctor lasts six years and for a paramedic three, so you do have to keep it in proportion. When I did my original hospital attachment at St Mary's in Paddington, one of my colleagues did get over enthusiastic and stitched a patient's mouth shut when treating a gash to his top lip, so we aren't necessarily of *ER* standard at all times.

But even with my medical training under my belt, I wasn't going to be an effective member of the troop until I'd got some operational experience and that wasn't too long in coming. We had a training deployment to Aden, which passed off without incident, but my first big test as an SAS soldier was to begin in February 1965 with the squadron's deployment on operations in Borneo.

CHAPTER FOUR

The Borneo confrontation kicked off way back in December 1962 with a revolt in Brunei against the rule of the hereditary Sultan. Brunei, Sabah and Sarawak were three old British colonies that made up the northern third of the island of Borneo, while the rest of the island (under the name Kalimantan) was ruled by Indonesia. At this time, Indonesia was ruled by President Sukarno, a nasty piece of work who had been in charge since the end of Dutch colonial rule without ever quite managing to introduce the democratic reforms he was always promising. With the British handing over power in Borneo, the three colonies were due to join the federation of Malaysia, along with Malaya and Singapore, but Sukarno rather fancied the idea of taking over himself, and was prepared to use any excuse to do so.

In fact, the trouble in 1962 was caused by local Bruneians and stemmed from all the usual reasons: more democracy; more money; and so on. But Sukarno was quite happy to give it a bit of support in order to try to up the ante. The upshot of this was that British troops who'd been brought in from Singapore to help stabilize things ended up staying in place, and this gave Sukarno an excuse to do the usual and start shouting on about anti-imperialism as a neat way of diverting attention from his problems at home.

Sukarno's next move was to send small incursions of Indonesian troops across the border to stir up trouble and discontent, to raid small villages, and to frighten the locals. This was a provocation that the British general in charge of operations in Borneo, Major General Walter Walker, couldn't ignore. Walker's problem was that he had a 900-mile jungle frontier to guard, as well as the prospect of an internal uprising and terrorist activity from a group called the 'Clandestine Communist Organization'. One of the options he was given was the use of an SAS squadron, and the result was that A Squadron went out to Borneo for the first time in January 1963.

Walker's original plan was to use A Squadron as a quick reaction force, parachuting them into the jungle to intercept Indonesian incursions inside friendly territory. Colonel Woodhouse quickly persuaded him that this wasn't such a tremendous use of their talents and instead they were deployed into remote jungle areas to befriend the local tribes and keep an eye on the border. The reasoning for this was sound: a four-man SAS patrol can only cover a certain amount of ground – and can only stay eyes down on a tiny patch of border – but once you get the locals on your side, you can get them working for you and they do a lot of the border surveillance for you. The other big benefit was that members of the jungle tribes were routinely crossing the border on hunting trips and visits to friends and relations, and they were ideal sources of intelligence on what the 'Indos' were up to.

Of course, at the beginning of operations in Borneo, 22 SAS consisted of just two operational squadrons, A and D, and this meant things became very tight in the Regiment because, along with training, the squadron that wasn't in Borneo was increasingly being called on to mount operations in Aden. The physical and mental strain of extended patrolling in the Borneo jungle was such that squadrons were restricted to four- or five-month tours and this meant very little rest time. To everybody's delight, the decision was made in early 1964, when I was still going through continuation training, to re-form B Squadron.

In effect, what happened was that the Regiment plucked some experienced NCOs out of the other two squadrons then ran some extra-large selection courses through the spring and summer of 1964. This meant that they were able to put together the nucleus of an operational squadron without compromising the standards that all the rest of us had been forced to meet. So no complaints there. While this was going on, our Aussie cousins were also building up their own SAS unit, with a view to deploying it in Borneo, and the Kiwis were doing much the same thing. So as 1964 continued, things were on the up for the Special Air Service.

It was also during 1964 that our role began to evolve from straightforward information reporting within 'British' Borneo to offensive intelligence gathering, attacks and ambushes across the border. Patrols were now tasked to cross the border covertly, investigating reports of Indonesian terrorist and special forces camps, in order to target them for larger, more conventional attacks. When we arrived in January 1965 things had moved on a bit, and the old hands in the squadron, now beginning their second tour in Borneo, were looking forward to some interesting operations. On the other hand, I had the tense, anxious excitement of someone about to lose his combat virginity.

The first thing that hits you when you arrive in a tropical area is the heat and damp: a wall of humidity that you walk into as you leave the air-conditioned interior of the plane. Then there's the smell: the rich, ripe, loamy scent of the jungle. The smell soon fades into the background but the humidity is always there, doubling the discomfort of everything you do, invading everything you have, rotting your clothing and rusting your equipment.

For the next four months we were to be based, when not in the jungle, in various places in and around the town of Kuching in the west of Sarawak. There were three locations: the old Palm Grove hotel, which was being rented by the army from a Chinese family and which accommodated various odds and sods as well as the SAS; some space in a hutted camp on the edge of town; and a place on 'Pea Green Road', which also housed our Ops set-up. Of course, being the SAS, we didn't have our own bed-space: in effect we operated on a 'hot-bunking' system – when we returned from a patrol or operation, we simply moved into the space vacated by someone who was going out on one.

At this point, the squadron was commanded by a major from the Devon and Dorsets called Roger Woodiwiss, a nice man with a very pukka accent and the right attitude for our kind of operations, but the squadron sergeant major, Bob Turnbull, was a legend in the Regiment. He had waited in the jungle, in the pouring rain, for days before successfully trapping a band of Communists and had won the Military Medal for gallantry. Anyway, for various reasons, there has always been a certain amount of informality in the SAS: the soldiers tend to be older and more experienced; we always work in very small groups where a formal hierarchy is superfluous; and, above all, part of the SAS philosophy is that discipline comes from within – officers and NCOs shouldn't have to impose it. This means that you often find troopers and junior NCOs calling senior ranks and sergeant majors by their Christian names or nicknames. But not Bob, or not in my case anyway, because I found that I instinctively called him

'Sir'. As for my patrol: there was Don Large in command, unflappable as ever; Nobby, a Scots lad; and Paddy Millikin, from southern Ireland via the Royal Signals, who was patrol signaller.

The first week or so after we arrived in Borneo was spent getting back into the swing of jungle operations: getting a feel for the ground and practising our immediate action drills, that sort of thing. This was the first time on operations in Borneo for me, Lofty and Paddy, but Nobby had been there before on D Squadron's last tour and he'd had a bit of a rough time. He'd been on patrol with Lofty Allen, Smoky Richardson and a young Irish lad called Paddy Condon when they'd accidentally crossed the border and stumbled into an Indo camp. Inevitably there was a bit of a kick-up as they tried to extricate themselves, and while they were breaking contact poor Paddy Condon got separated, wounded and captured. This was a disaster for him, because the Indos tortured then murdered him, but it dropped the rest of the patrol in the shit as well because Paddy had the radio.

Well, this had left Smoky, Lofty and Nobby in a bad situation. They knew they were caught up in a complex of Indo camps – and from what they'd seen, it could have held anything up to 150 or so soldiers and terrorists – and because they were lost, the only sure way they had of getting out was to retrace their steps, which would have been madness now because they were compromised. In the end, after several days, creeping about in the thick jungle, during which they also searched for Paddy but failed to find him, they made it to a heli-landing site and were lifted out. The stress and exhaustion of this situation had been enough to put Nobby in hospital for a couple of weeks to recover and there was no question that he was still a bit twitchy.

During the next few months, the Indos had also killed Billy

White from D Squadron and Buddha Bexton from A Squadron in separate incidents, so we were under no illusions that operations were going to be easy. With his usual thoroughness, Lofty was damned certain we were going to be properly prepared. So when our first tasking came up – my first real live operation with the Regiment – I was pretty much confident I was ready for it.

We had a standard routine for operations. Lofty would get his briefing and prepare his orders whilst the rest of us got the basics sorted out: kit preparation, checking the radio worked, that kind of thing. Then Lofty gave his orders, and afterwards we could crack on with specific things that we would need for this operation, get our rations broken down, test-fire weapons, and rehearse patrol drills ready for the off.

The first operation turned out to be a recce of the area between the Koemba and Sekayan rivers, looking for routes and tracks that might be useful for future cross-border operations, and nosing around a village called Kapoet where there was meant to be some kind of Indonesian special forces patrol base. Our patrol was teamed with Alec Spence and Joe Lock's patrols so that we could cover more ground, and maybe support each other if the shit hit the fan. The idea was that we'd cross the border mob-handed, establish a patrol base of sorts, which would be manned by Joe's boys, while Alec's and our team went off to do our tasks. The plan was that we were going to stay there for fourteen days, then we'd reunite and re-cross the border as a big gang ready for our pick-up. Before we left, the OC took Lofty to one side and briefed him.

'You've got one new boy; you've got one nervous wreck; and you've got Millikin. If anything starts to go wrong, don't hang around, just bring 'em straight out . . .'

Well, that was understandable, in my case anyway. I was

very much the untested member of the patrol having never served on operations with the Regiment; and it would be hard not to be a bit anxious if you'd been through an experience like Nobby's, but to know why the Boss was worried about Paddy you really had to see him. I don't go in for all this cobblers about the Irish but Paddy Millikin *did* look like a pantomime Irishman. Five foot nine inches tall, black-haired, brown-toothed and thin, he was perpetually scruffy and dirty – in uniform anyway – making a shirt last three days where we'd all change after one. He spoke with an Irish brogue as thick as porridge, and in the field he bumbled about apparently oblivious to any kind of danger, with his personal kit jumbled about in a mess we referred to as 'Bergen pie'.

But appearances can be deceptive: Paddy had actually been with the Regiment since before the Jebel Akhdar campaign in 1958, having originally come in as a member of 264 SAS Signals Squadron, and although he'd only done selection fairly recently, he had a good deal of experience under his belt. Even better, those of us who worked with him knew him to be the most talented signaller in the Regiment, capable of getting through in conditions where many in his position wouldn't have bothered trying.

With everything ready, we flew into a border LZ in a helicopter and, after shaking out, crossed the border and began heading south-west at a steady patrol pace. As soon as we left the clearing, the jungle canopy folded around us and we were absorbed into the strange twilight of the ancient rainforest.

Most people are surprised the first time they go into the jungle at how dark it is and how noisy it can be. When the first lads from the Regiment had travelled out in 1963, the local commander had insisted that they stop off for a few days in Singapore to try to develop a bit of a tan so they wouldn't stand out amongst other troops: what he didn't realize was that soldiers who spend any length of time in the jungle invariably turn as white as ghosts because of the complete absence of direct sunlight. Now, as we headed into Indonesian territory, I was trying to remember the lessons of the jungle warfare course: trying to stay alert; trying to look through the trees rather than at them; trying to spot any movement or sign that shouldn't have been there.

Most soldiers find the jungle a very hostile environment. You move very slowly because it isn't safe to use ridges, rivers, tracks and paths; you're constantly wet from sweat, rain and humidity, and this means that your skin chafes and your feet rot; and you're under constant attacks from insects, leeches and even the occasional snake. We even had to strain our tea though our teeth to avoid swallowing all the insects swimming in it. Around 1900 hours, when the sun goes down, you stop entirely because it's pitch black. Underneath the thick jungle canopy, you can hardly see your hand in front of your face, but you can hear all kinds of strange noises – insects, monkeys and birds, squeaking, hooting, jabbering and crashing around amongst the trees – which can terrify the uninitiated. Even during the day it's dark and gloomy most of the time, except when occasional shafts of sunlight pierce through the leaves and branches above, casting impenetrable shadows. We basked in these rare rays of sunshine, drying out our clothes as best we could. Paddy would open the radio and try to dry it out. The thick vegetation on the ground means it's rare you can see more than fifteen or twenty metres at best: you can never be sure that you aren't being watched by an enemy lying in ambush.

Worst of all though were the loads we had to carry. We weren't at war with Indonesia, it was a 'confrontation', and that meant that British forces could not overtly cross the border. When we went in to Indonesia, we went on our own, carrying everything with us.

Of course, it helps to have someone like Lofty leading the patrol when you're on your first time out. Unlike a lot of patrol commanders, Lofty also acted as the lead scout with me as his number two, covering his back. I reckoned this was a small advantage because if we did bump into any enemy, chances were that Lofty was so big and frightening they'd try to nail him first rather than go for me. But it also meant we operated at Lofty's speed, and that was a tremendous advantage.

The thing about Lofty – the secret of his success – is his laid-back attitude. He's not lazy – that's the last thing you could accuse him of – but he's not bothered about doing things quickly for quickly's sake. He knew that in the jungle you have to go slowly. For instance, walking alone you'd easily get caught up by these atap thorns – wait-a-whiles we called them. Struggle and they'd dig deeper in. Stop and carefully disentangle yourself and you'd be all right.

The Borneo jungle is good jungle in many ways, clean and reasonably easy to move through, but it has its own hazards. One of these is that the ground tends to be very broken: beneath the canopy there are a lot of ravines, gullies, cliffs and ridges; and like most jungle areas I've been to, there was a lot of crap on the ground, ranging from tangles of creeper and leaf litter up to massive dead tree trunks. Lofty was brought up in the country – as a boy he practically lived in the woods – and while the Forest of Dean isn't the Borneo jungle, he had the woodsman's knack of spotting tracks and paths that most of us wouldn't see. He also had experience in Korea, Malaya, Oman and everywhere else he'd been, and he knew how quickly operations go tits-up if you don't operate in a cool and professional manner. So we went along at a steady pace, stopping when we needed to and getting the job done without hassle or mock heroics. All the time we'd be constantly monitoring our surroundings, pointing out emergency RVs and good landing spots. One of the reasons the SAS is so professional is that they fully understand the need for good intelligence.

The first night we followed a long, gently rising spur up on to a high ridge from which we set up the RV Joe Lock's patrol would operate, and the next day, the three patrols did clearance recces to make sure the entire area was free of the enemy, which it was. Then, after spending the night at the RV, we set off the next morning to complete our task.

But we didn't get very far. A couple of thousand metres past the limit of our clearance patrols the previous day, we had found ourselves at the top of a cliff-face some 250 to 300 metres high, a cliff-face that wasn't marked on any of our maps. We recced about 1,000 metres in either direction but couldn't find a way down and so, with evening drawing on, we basha'd* up for the night.

Next morning Lofty and I left our Bergens with Nobby and Paddy and headed off along the cliff top in our belt order† in the hope of finding a route down. We'd covered about a mile when I saw Lofty pause then signal to me to get down. I slowly sank to the ground, wondering what he'd seen, and then I noticed it too: a hundred metres or so in front of us there was a great crashing and commotion going on in the trees, as something large and presumably unpleasant made its way towards us at high speed. I was wondering if it was an elephant or even a buffalo when I saw Lofty point upwards, and we watched as two huge ginger orang-utans chased each

* *Basha*: shelter (Malay).
† Belt order: escape belts containing water-bottles, an emergency medical pack, rations, ammunition, compass and parang. We slept with them on.

other through the treetops, swinging from branch to branch and hooting raucously.

Well, not something you see every day, even if you are patrolling in deep jungle. In fact, by this time the squadron had already adopted a pet monkey (called 'Scholey' for some strange reason!) but it was only small; the big apes were a rare sight. One other encounter took place on a later operation when the patrol were being winched out of the jungle. I was coming up through the canopy when a problem developed with the winch and the crewman indicated that I should unhook myself and step onto a thick branch about 200 feet above the ground while it was fixed. As I was sitting there, I noticed a large irate-looking orang-utan staring at me, and as I watched he began to become more and more agitated, obviously pissed off that some SAS trooper had invaded his personal living space. After a few minutes of hard staring, the huge ape suddenly came straight at me, scuttling very nimbly along the branches. Perched precariously 200 feet up and faced with 400 pounds of orange-furred muscle power, I did the only thing I could: I shot it.

Even though I was carrying a Sterling SMG fitted with a silencer, the sound of a shot caused consternation down below, and this was compounded when the rest of the patrol heard the crashing of a body tumbling down through the branches. Catching a fleeting glimpse of an apparently human form dropping from the trees, Kevin, one of the guys in the patrol, got underneath it to catch it – or at least to break its fall. Instead he wound up lying underneath a quarter of a ton of warm, dead ape. The usual near silent patrol routine went for a ball of chalk.

'Jesus Christ! Get this fuckin' thing off me!'

The rest of the team grabbed the orang-utan to haul it off and found they had to walk a few metres just to straighten its arms out.

Once everything was sorted out, we decided to take the orang-utan down to the local aboriginal kampong to see if they wanted to eat it. This also proved to be a mistake: to the locals, the orang-utans were pretty much regarded as sacred, and they certainly wouldn't dream of scoffing one. It took a load of chocolate and meat blocks from the patrol's ration packs to straighten them out. A good lesson learned for the whole Regiment.

Not that Lofty and I had any plans to shoot the orang-utans that we'd seen on this occasion but it is good to be aware of the consequences of that kind of act, not the least of which is a great big dead ginger-haired monkey dropping on you from a considerable height.

Scholey the monkey became quite a popular member of the squadron, so much so that it was eventually decided to take him parachuting and award him his 'wings', which is where disaster eventually struck. The first few jumps went okay – he didn't seem to mind the experience at all – but it all went wrong on his last descent when he heard me coughing. Unfortunately, we used to communicate with him by making these sort of coughing, grunting noises so the sound obviously confused him. The upshot was that he started to climb the rigging lines of his chute, partially collapsed it, plopped into a river next to the DZ, unravelled himself from the harness, swam ashore and made off into the jungle, jabbering frantically. RTU* one monkey.

We finished our exploration for that day and headed back to our RV with Nobby and Paddy. Lofty found a decent basha site and we began to get settled in for the night. The army has a saying, 'Any fool can be uncomfortable', and that's just as true for the SAS as it is for some rear-echelon desk driver.

* Return to Unit.

The rations we carried were the standard army compo of the time: meat blocks, packets of rice, boiled sweets, brew kit, that kind of thing; but because we were going to be out for fourteen days, there was no possible way we could carry the contents of fourteen full ration packs and keep our Bergens under fifty-five pounds, which was the squadron limit at that time. So we'd break the rations down, select the bits we liked, bin the bits we didn't, and fill the gaps with little extras to make what we took taste better. Everyone carried curry powder to add to their rice and meat, but lots of the lads might take a few small onions, or even some *ikon billis* which were small dried fish much favoured by the locals and the old Malaya hands from the regiment. They stank like old manure before you cooked them, but when you boiled them up with your curry they were rather pleasant, and certainly made a change from compo.

The patrolling we did was physically and mentally demanding so when we stopped for the day, although we couldn't switch off, we always made an effort to relax as much as the operational situation allowed. We would put up our bashas, cook our scoff and send off our sitrep (situation report) while it was still light, which meant we could get into the night-time routine, alternating sleeping with keeping a watch, as smoothly as possible. It also meant that everything was squared away when night fell. In equatorial regions you don't get much twilight. It's dark very soon after the sun sets and down under the canopy it's absolutely pitch black.

Basha'ing up at this time was fairly easy, because Lofty had got hold of a great big piece of polythene from Dick Cooper, one of the other patrol commanders. This was about the size of my living room and Dick had painted leaves and streaks all over it to camouflage it, creating a nice big water proof cover for the whole patrol that we could string up in the trees to protect us for the night. This left all of us happy, with the exception of Nobby who had insisted on doing his own clearance patrol round the area and reckoned we might as well have put up a lighthouse to advertise our presence. Despite his jitters, we overruled him and while Paddy and I got the scoff going, he went to escort Lofty while he was having his evening dump.

We were getting the curry under way when Paddy noticed a huge pig-fly settling on the underside of the polythene, just near where he was peeling an onion with his fighting knife. Without thinking he flicked at the fly with the sharp end. Disaster! He missed the fly and cut a two-foot slit through Lofty's prized 'super-basha'.

'Oh, Jesus Christ! Quick, Pete, pass me some masking tape and for God's sake don't tell Lofty!'

I passed a roll of tape over and he made a quick repair before Lofty returned with Nobby. It was getting dark now and we were lying under the basha eating our curry while Lofty wrote out the patrol sitrep for Paddy to send out. It was also pissing down with rain outside, but we were all secure and dry under the polythene. Well, temporarily: as the rain continued, Nobby, Paddy and I watched a bulge growing in the polythene just where the masking tape was placed, which happened to be above where Lofty was lying down, having a last fag before turning in. Suddenly *splosh*! The masking tape gave way and the water emptied all over Lofty. In a flash, Lofty was up, brushing water off himself, effing and blinding, and cursing the polythene sheet. Almost as quickly, Paddy was there helping him, rapidly seizing the opportunity to remove the evidence of the masking tape.

'Bloody thing must have split,' moaned Lofty.

'I'm sure you're right, Loft,' agreed Paddy, making frantic

hand signals to me. We sorted ourselves out and settled down again.

Next day we continued with our recces along the cliff-top – and the next, and the next – until we ran out of time. Then we began the trek back to our step-up RV and the other two patrols. It had been very frustrating: we'd followed hundreds of animal tracks which seemed likely to lead us to a route down the cliff, but each one had petered out after a few metres. Quite often, we could see rain glinting on the hut roofs of our target, Kapoet, a few kilometres from where we stood, but there was no way for us to reach it.

We made it back to the RV and met up with the other patrols without any bother, and began preparations for the trip back over the border. By now, at the end of the patrol, we were getting pretty short on food. This wasn't a problem for most of us – we had enough to keep going for the last day or so – but poor old Lofty was getting a bit desperate. The fifty-five pound weight limit was being rigorously enforced, but being a man mountain he needed more food than most to keep going, and he'd also had the experience of two years' starvation rations in his POW camp. So Lofty was not entirely happy at running out of scoff.

But he did have plenty of fags, and this gave him an idea. Alec Spence is only a little bloke so he still had a fair amount of scoff in his Bergen, but he was trying to pack in smoking, and hadn't taken any cigarettes with him, while Lofty – a chain smoker – still had a fair few left. Lofty got a little way upwind of Alec and lit up, and in no time flat Alec was gagging for a smoke. Very soon, a deal was done and Lofty was filling his face while Alec filled his lungs.

We crossed the border without incident and lifted out to our base at Kuching for a couple of days' relaxation before being retasked. To nobody's great surprise, we were to be sent back to the same area, once again trying to find a route to the supposed special forces camp at Kapoet. This time, we had the benefit of experience from our previous patrol – as well as Alec's, which had found a route down from the plateau where we'd found ourselves – and the approach phase of the patrol was no big problem. When we got close to Kapoet Lofty decided that the best way to handle the target phase would be for us to cache our Bergens and get the whole recce over with quickly, rather than spend several days hanging around an area that was likely to be relatively thickly populated.

Well, this struck me as sensible, but Nobby was none too happy. On his previous tour he'd been compromised in just this kind of area, and he was very wary of repeating the experience. Nevertheless, he eventually agreed to go along with it and off we set.

We cached our Bergens and approached the village from the north, moving quickly with all our senses on maximum alert. We reached the river and found a crossing a few yards up from an old disused fish-trap, then moved into thick secondary jungle to the east of the village through which we could travel quickly and without too much risk of compromise. After a quarter of an hour or so we came to the edge of the jungle on some slightly higher ground from where we were able to see straight into the village, about half a kilometre away. We sat quietly for half an hour or so, scanning for any sign of movement or life, but as far as any of us could tell, the whole place was dead.

We moved off as rain began to fall, carefully making our way closer to the village through new secondary jungle. If this was the site of a special forces base, we could be damned sure that this kind of area would be mined or booby-trapped at least, and our nerves were now stretched to breaking point. However, we got through without incident and arrived at the riverbank opposite the village itself. Lofty made his way into a position where he could do a binocular recce of the village while the rest of us deployed to cover him.

And then Nobby cracked.

On his last tour he'd found himself accidentally on the wrong side of the border, being hunted down by Indo special forces, with one member of his patrol missing and probably dead. Now he was deliberately crossing the border to try to find the same enemy and I guess the tension was just too much for him. All he wanted to do was to get away from the danger. Unfortunately, there was nowhere for him to go.

By now, we had a good idea that there was nobody about but Lofty needed to be sure, so the next move was to try to calm Nobby down while he went off to check. He was away on his own for forty minutes or so, poking around as the rain got steadily heavier, while we tried to maintain a watch on what was going on around us and talk Nobby out of his state of terror. By the time Lofty returned, Nobby had calmed down enough that we didn't need to hold him down, but he was still in no state to operate effectively. It wasn't that he was paralysed with fright so much as that he'd just decided enough was enough. 'They're all around us,' he kept saying, 'we're surrounded.'

When he got back, Lofty briefed us that he still hadn't seen any movement or sign of life in the village, but that he hadn't covered all the ground because he'd been on his own with no back-up. Then he proposed that he would patrol along the riverbank, in full view of the village, in the hope of drawing fire, while we covered him from the jungle. This may sound foolhardy, but it wasn't completely mad because it was pissing down with rain, visibility was fairly poor and troops operating in the jungle rarely have their weapons zeroed for long ranges: most engagements take place at around twenty to thirty metres range and weapons are generally fired instinctively. Lofty was hoping that any enemy in the village would see him, but he knew that at the 400 or so metres range, they weren't going to hit him unless they got very lucky. Well, we all thought it was a reasonable enough plan, except for Nobby. The idea of deliberately trying to attract the enemy's attention wasn't his current idea of a good day out. His past experiences had made him apprehensive and now he was arguing that Lofty's plan made no tactical sense.

Eventually Lofty lost patience. 'If you don't get a move on I'll stuff this barrel up your nose and blow your brains out!'

Not surprisingly, Nobby gave in.

We carried on with the patrol, but nothing stirred and, after Lofty had walked several hundred metres in full view of the village, we headed back into the jungle, making our way towards the Bergen cache. Or so we thought. Lofty was a brilliant jungle navigator, but somehow or other he managed to get us lost this time. We farted around for nearly an hour, with Lofty hacking away at a big stand of *ladang* – tall thick bulrushes – before we stopped, sat down, and Lofty had a fag, got his map out and methodically worked out what had gone wrong.

It seemed that he had mistaken a fish trap in the river for the one we had seen on the way into the village. Lofty did a few calculations, found where we actually were and led off again into the relative safety of the primary jungle. Unfortunately, night was falling and there was no chance of getting to the Bergen cache before it became too dark to operate. Instead, we stopped in a suitable bit of cover, and tried to get what sleep we could in the freezing rain with nothing but leaves to shelter us.

Next morning, at first light, Lofty led us straight to the Bergen cache but before we could settle down, he took me off to do a clearance patrol round the area, leaving the other two with the packs. We didn't find anything untoward but somehow, probably the result of exhaustion, we got lost again, even though we knew we were no real distance from the cache. Patrol standard operating procedure (SOP) in this case was straightforward: hoot like an owl and home in on the reply. We stood still and Lofty clearly but softly called, 'Woo-hoo.'

There was no response. A little louder this time, 'Woo-hoo!'

Still no response. Even louder, 'Woo-hoo!!'

Nothing. What we didn't realize was that the other two had heard us perfectly well but that Nobby wouldn't let Paddy answer in case 'they' heard them. Now Lofty was pissed off.

'WOO-fucking-HOO!!!'

At the sound of this tremendous shout, all the birds in hearing range took off in fright.

The response came from close by and we rejoined them.

As we arrived at the basha, Nobby looked up and said, 'Oh, good, it's you. Let's have a quick brew and get out of here then.' And certainly the SOP now should have been to press on back to the border in order to evade any follow-up that might have started, but we were shagged out and Lofty made a judgement call, deciding that we would lie up that day to rest and eat, get back in shape and make sure that when we did the exfiltration we'd be firing on all cylinders. We moved a little way from where we'd left the Bergens, sorted ourselves out, sent off the patrol sitrep and settled down.

Next morning we were in much better condition, and the move back to the border was accomplished in good time. The plan was that we should RV with the other two patrols at the LZ, but it was our task to make sure that the LZ itself was clear. We'd been told in the sitrep from base that the area was free of British troops but we hadn't been at the RV long when

Lofty spotted movement and saw two small local tribesmen dressed in jungle greens and carrying pump-action shotguns. They were wearing the recognition sign of the Border Scouts – a white strip sewn round their hats – and they were immediately followed by a platoon of Scots Guards. Almost at the moment they emerged into the clearing, Tak – Joe Lock's fearsome looking Fijian lead scout – appeared from the opposite direction. Fortunately, both sides spotted Lofty and no harm was done, but it was a sticky moment for everybody.

Alec and his boys turned up a little later and we lifted out for debrief back in Kuching. By now Nobby was much calmer, but it was obvious that there was no point in his carrying on with the Regiment, or the army for that matter. There were two ways forward: a formal report from Lofty followed by official action to expel him, or a quiet word here and there to enable him to get out without a cloud hanging over him. Not surprisingly, Nobby went for the second option, using an old injury to show that he was medically unfit for further operations. It was a shame, really, because he was a nice bloke, but he'd had to face more than he could take and the stress became too much. He wasn't the first SAS man to break down under those circumstances, and he wasn't the last.

Back in Kuching, the lads were having a laugh at the expense of one of the young officers who'd recently joined the squadron, a guy called Robin Letts. He'd gone off on a patrol with Taff Springles and they'd called in at a tribal kampong on the way back to make sure that everyone was OK and do a bit of 'hearts and minds' work. These kampongs consisted of a wooden longhouse on stilts – where the tribe all lived, cooked, ate and slept – with an interesting method of waste disposal. The floor of the longhouse had big gaps in it and all the left-over food and rubbish was dropped down through the holes where it was devoured by a herd of wild pigs below. Just before the patrol left the kampong, Robin asked Taff if he had any bog-paper left in his ration pack. Taff gave him a few sheets but told him, 'You won't need it.'

'Why not?'

'You'll see.'

Robin sloped off into the undergrowth, dropped his kecks and got down to business. A few moments later there was an anguished shout: 'Get away from me, you filthy beasts!'

Seconds afterwards, Robin emerged from the bushes with his trousers round his ankles pursued by a selection of kampong pigs, one of whom had started to eat Robin's turd as it emerged. When they'd finished laughing, Taff graciously offered to demonstrate how it should be done. He climbed a tree, hung his arse over a branch and let fly. As it happened, Taff's turd dropped into a thick patch of undergrowth and although the pigs could smell it, they couldn't find it. Taff helped them out as they rootled amongst the leaf-mould: 'Warm . . . you're getting warmer . . .'

The next tasking we had was a little unusual. An Australian infantry battalion was coming out to relieve one of the Gurkha battalions as part of the Commonwealth effort and would be moving into a notoriously hot sector of the front. As a result, the whole squadron was to be deployed over the border as a screen to give the Aussies early warning in the event that the Indos decided to make a move while they were still settling in. With Nobby gone, we needed a replacement in the patrol and somehow or other the system coughed up Bert Perkins, one of my instructors in jungle training. This ex-Gloster had been captured with Lofty in Korea. Shortly before we were due to go into the jungle, Paddy's appendix flared up and he got hauled off to hospital for an appendectomy at somewhat short notice, so he was replaced temporarily by Jock Griffin.

In fact, with one exception, it was a very quiet and almost restful operation. We didn't have anything much to do except sit and wait for the Indos – and they didn't show up, except for one brief moment literally a few minutes after we'd crossed the border. I don't know why, but for some reason the headshed, the bloke in charge, had specified that on this job we had to send off a signal as soon as we were over the border, which, where we crossed it, was marked by a river. We got ourselves across and found a suitable place to stop while Jock, the signaller, got set up and did his stuff. While we were waiting, Bert and I had to keep a look-out because the other two would be busy and, having tried a couple of positions which weren't really suitable, I was just shifting into a good spot when I sensed something wrong behind me.

I slowly turned round and immediately noticed that the others had frozen: Jock Griffin was sitting with his back to a tree and the Morse key on his lap, his face white as a sheet; Bert was poised in a crouch with his rifle in the aim; Lofty, just in front of me, was staring intently into the undergrowth a few feet away. Then I saw it. Not more than five metres away, through the foliage, I could see the boots and lower legs of soldiers walking slowly past. A platoon of Indos doing a border patrol.

We stayed as quiet as we could as they passed us, hardly daring to breathe let alone move until they were well clear, then we let out loud sighs of relief. Lofty was the first to speak. 'Pete, what the bloody hell are you doing standing there? You should've been covering your bloody arcs.'

I couldn't resist it. 'Your orders Lofty.'

'What do you mean?'

'You've always said, "If the shit ever hits the fan, get behind something thick," so I got behind you.'

'You cheeky bugger!'

The biggest benefit I got from that patrol was spending time with Bert Perkins. Although I'd done the patrol medic course, Bert had been doing the job for years and really knew his stuff. We spent a lot of our time going through the medical pack with him showing me various tricks of the trade, so much so that at the end of the two week deployment I felt as if I'd done a postgraduate medical cadre.

Back in Kuching we got a permanent replacement for Jock in the distinctly misshapen form of another ex-member of the Parachute Regiment, Kevin Walsh, a man with a face like the last date in an Arab's knapsack, widely known as the airborne wart. Now Kevin has had a bit of a mixed press in the Regiment over the years, mainly because his sense of humour rarely coincided with that of the hierarchy. On one occasion we were doing a classroom map exercise in Hereford and Willy Fyfe, our young and impressionable troop commander, came up with the following scenario. 'Corporal Walsh, we're on an operation, doing an evasion, and you fall and break your leg. There's no way you can keep up with us and we're short on ammunition and rations. I decide that the rest of the patrol must continue onwards so we leave you with two rounds of ammunition and enough food and water for forty-eight hours. What would you do?'

Kev thought about this for a moment and then replied, 'Sir, as you walked away from me, I'd put both rounds right between your fuckin' shoulder-blades.'

He'd been on the selection course before mine but there had been a delay on his joining the squadron because at the end of his jungle training he'd nearly managed to chop his own leg off with a parang. He'd been kicking his heels in hospital then recovering in Hereford while we were training in Aden and had only come to join us a few weeks into the Borneo deployment. He'd taken part in several patrols with different teams, all of which had gone slightly wrong and wound up with them being chased out by the Indos. By the time he got to us, as well as being short, ugly and northern – I forgot to mention he was a Yorkshire lad* – he also had the reputation of being a Jonah.

Rumour had it that the only time anyone had been pleased to see him was a few weeks before when a patrol led by Geordie Lillico had walked into a platoon of Indos. Geordie got hit through the thigh, which blew a big hole in his back, while Jock Thompson, his lead scout, got one in the leg, breaking his femur and severing his femoral artery. Geordie and Jock had put down enough fire to blunt any immediate threat and get themselves – just about – clear of the area, but they were in deep shit: severely wounded, separated from the rest of the patrol who'd followed the Regiment's 'shoot and scoot' drill and made it back to their previous RV, and cut off behind enemy lines.

A search was mounted, more in hope than expectation, involving helicopters, the local Gurkha battalion and several nearby SAS patrols (we were on patrol at the time and Lofty had offered our services when Geordie's patrol had disappeared off the net, but we were too far away to be any help). It was Kevin who'd found Jock, stoned out of his mind on morphine he'd pinched from the dispensary and half dead from loss of blood after he'd crawled nearly a mile with his leg hanging off. Jock's a tough little bugger, though: the shock of seeing Kevin's face after an ordeal like that would have

---

* Any speech by Kevin should be immediately translated into a strong Yorkshire whine.

been enough to finish most people off. Thankfully, Geordie also made it. It would have been a terrible thing to have deprived the Regiment of his fun-loving, laid-back, easy-going approach to life.

So, as it happened, the first time that the newly formed team of Large, Scholey, Millikin and Walsh had the opportunity to test their collective abilities was on yet another recce in the direction of Kapoet and the rumoured special forces camp. Once again we went through all the preparations over several days, and although it was a familiar routine by now, we didn't cut any corners.

Over my twenty-odd years in the Regiment, a lot of people have asked me, 'So what makes the SAS so special, then?' (with varying amounts of scepticism and aggression, normally relating to how much they've had to drink). My answer has usually been something along the lines of: 'The SAS is no better or worse than any other part of the army. It simply has a particular role that not every soldier is suitable for, blah, blah, blah.' (Scholey, ever the diplomat!) But that isn't really true. The thing that marks the SAS out from the rest of the army is the meticulousness of its approach to everything it does. There's no point in mounting operations that don't work: it's a waste of time, money and, above all, lives, and the SAS has never had enough of any of those commodities to throw them away. Every time we went out to do the job, we made damn sure we were prepared and ready for it.

Which is not to say that we were fanatics. While we were getting ready for this operation, Alec Spence was chatting with Lofty and told him, 'I wouldn't go out with any one of the three blokes in your patrol, mate, let alone all fucking three of them!' Lofty told me later that he'd thought about this and come to the conclusion that the only thing likely to happen was that we'd all die laughing at some cock-up or other. This was true enough. I only have three memories of that particular patrol: when we arrived at the border LZ prior to crossing, we found that it was a company patrol base manned by a Guards unit. As we were sorting ourselves out, Lofty was ushered away by some character, and we were taken off to a little 12 x 12 tent and given a meal. Well that was very nice, but it later transpired that Lofty had been to the sergeants' mess for the full works: a three course lunch with coffee afterwards! You can imagine the hard time we gave him after that. Throughout the patrol we made him eat separately, labelling his part of the basha as the 'sergeants' mess' revenge.

Once we got ourselves over to the Indo side of the border, the hilarity level dropped a little bit, but even so it was never far from the surface. At the bottom of the border ridge, right in the area which was usually heavily patrolled by the Indonesians and which required maximum stealth, there was a stream about eighteen inches deep and six or seven feet across. At six foot five Lofty could leap across it with ease; at five foot ten it wasn't too hard for me to follow him; at five nine Paddy made short work of it; but as Lofty and I made our way forward to see what was going on up ahead, all we heard was the splash of the airborne wart hitting the water, followed by the unmistakable sound of poorly suppressed hysterical laughter. We returned to find Paddy curled up laughing while Kevin, effing and blinding at him, was covered from head to toe in water and stinking mud. As he'd made the jump, his feet had caught in a tree root and he'd fallen flat on his face into the stream, then found that his ankles were so caught up that the only way he could get his face out was by doing press-ups.

Later on in the patrol, he was the victim of another unfortunate incident after Paddy had gone off to lay his evening 'egg'. After he had finished he was rabbiting away in his usual fashion: 'Ah, now, that's better, I've been a bit blocked up but I'm all clear now. . .' et cetera, et cetera, as he busied himself round the basha. Suddenly, Kevin spoke up: 'What's that fuckin' 'orrible smell?'

He sniffed around a bit, then groaned: 'You fuckin' dirty Irish bastard! I'm all covered in your shit!' Poor old Kevin. When Paddy had finished his dump he'd managed to step in it and then trodden it all over Kevin's part of the basha; Kevin had then sat down in it and managed to get it all over himself.

Something about Kevin seemed to attract these incidents. Later in the year when we were back in the UK we were exercising round mid-Wales in the Pinkies. The weather was awful and, because the Pinkies are completely open to the elements, we were wearing big, thick, quilted 'tank suits' to keep out the cold. Kevin had been on the piss the night before and was suffering a bit, and after we'd been driving for an hour or so he piped up: 'Lofty, we've got to stop so's I can have a dump or I'll shit myself.' We pulled over and Kev hopped out into the bushes, rapidly undoing the fasteners to get the tank suit off. There was a bit of rustling and the odd satisfied remark, 'Thank God for that', and that sort of thing.

After a few minutes, Lofty called out, 'Come on, Kevin, aren't you finished yet?'

'Keep your hair on, Lofty, I'm just coming . . .' There was a pause and a loud moan. 'FOR FUCK'S SAKE! . . . I don't fucking believe it!'

'What's the matter, Kev?'

'I've shat in me hood.'

Three weeks before the end of the Borneo tour, a new job came up for the patrol. This time the idea was to cross the border into Kalimantan then try to locate the river Koemba near a village called Poeri. This had been attempted by at least five previous patrols from both D and A Squadrons and none of them had made it, mainly because the area seemed to be largely surrounded by swamps. Major Woodiwiss, the squadron commander, had had to return to Hereford because his wife was having complications having a baby, but he had briefed Lofty that this was a high priority, and Lofty was determined to see it through.

There was a fair amount of excitement in the headshed about the operation because Intelligence was sure that the special forces base, which we'd looked for but never found near Kapoet, was getting its resupply by river. Brigade command's view was that if we could maintain a covert observation post on the river we would be able to confirm this, and that if we subsequently put in an ambush, we would certainly disrupt – and maybe even close down – their operations in this sector of the border.

Preparation was intense: we read the previous patrols' reports, studied aerial photographs, and looked at all the mapping. Then, as usual, we carried out thorough rehearsals of the physical side of the operation, our patrol drills and standard operating procedures: making sure we were all practised in RV and bug-out drills (where you need to break contact with the enemy and fire while moving back); obstacle crossing; and all the other little details that mean the difference between success and failure. Communications were going to be the usual high-speed Morse code using an HF '128' set – a great heavy thing when you included all the batteries and other bits and pieces – and while Paddy Millikin got on with sorting that out we carried out our own preparations. As the patrol medic I had to be prepared to deal with any combat injuries we experienced, as well as treating the various illnesses and problems that can set in very quickly in that harsh environment. But we all double-checked each other's preparations as well. If we'd lost Paddy, for example, another of us would have to take over the radio, so we all needed to be confident that it worked; if I was wounded, I'd have a job treating myself, so the other boys needed to know what goodies were in the medical kit and what to do with them. This may seem pedantic, but it's the only way to operate successfully in the long term, and it's worth remembering that the real problem with the Bravo Two Zero patrol in the Gulf was that when they reached Iraq, they found that their radios didn't work and they had no way of getting back or calling for help. Proper checks by every member of the patrol might well have prevented this happening.

On this operation, I was carrying sixteen days' rations for myself, as well as the patrol medical pack, a SARBE* and my own kit, plus two days' worth of rations for Paddy Millikin who had to carry the heavy radio. Not a lot of room for personal kit as you can see, which meant that the dinner jacket had to stay home.

Spending a lot of time on this kind of operation puts you under a huge amount of pressure – stress, we'd call it now – and before we set off, Lofty took me to one side and asked me if I wanted to drop out. I'd done a lot of patrolling in the past few months and, apparently, Major Woodiwiss thought I'd spent enough time in the jungle for one tour. I told Lofty 'Bollocks!' and it was left at that, though actually Paddy was more of a worry than I was, because he'd had his appendix taken out fairly recently and hadn't had a great deal of time to recuperate.

* Search and Rescue Beacon.

With our kit packed and squared away, we just had to wait for the vehicle that was bringing our weapons from the armoury and taking us on to the airfield where we were due to get a Twin Pioneer helicopter flight up to our forward mounting base, and it was now I hit a snag. For some reason the clowns at the armoury had sent the wrong rifle. The rest of the lads had their normal weapons, but I got one that I hadn't had a chance to zero-in or even test-fire. This was really annoying, and also a little worrying: you need to have confidence in your weapon because your life may depend on it, and my usual rifle had never let me down in months of training and operations. As the number-two man in the patrol, my job involved protecting the leader, who would be busy with navigation and route-finding, and he needed to know that he could depend on me to engage any enemy he hadn't seen. I spent the whole twenty-minute flight stripping, cleaning and reassembling the rifle, and although Don told me that I'd get a chance to test-fire it at the forward mounting base, I still wasn't happy.

Sure enough, when we arrived there twenty minutes later, there was already a helicopter 'burning and turning', waiting to take us off to the LZ from where we were to cross the border. Cursing, I ran to it holding on to my Bergen and the suspect rifle, and from there we were whisked off to the border where we were met by a platoon of Argyll and Sutherland Highlanders.

The Jocks' job was to escort us a short distance over the border then head back to friendly territory, and this they did, leaving us on our own, and me very unhappy about this potentially duff rifle. We moved off at a wary pace, heading west of our true objective for the rest of that day. When we'd put a bit of space between us and the border, we basha'd up. This gave the rest of the patrol the opportunity to give my rifle the once-over and try to reassure me and, to be fair, I couldn't see anything wrong with it myself, but I was still uneasy, and I set the regulator to zero so there was no chance of a gas stoppage.

The next day we continued on the same route. We didn't want to head straight for our objective for one simple reason: tracks. No matter how good you are in the jungle, you inevitably leave tracks that can be followed and we didn't want to give away our target by making a beeline straight for it. Instead, we would aim off until we reached a recognizable point, then close in from there. Not only did this preserve our operational security, but it would also make navigation easier in the final stages of our approach.

It was during the second day that we came across our first sign of the enemy. As we slowly pushed through the undergrowth, Lofty suddenly signalled us to stop. We froze initially, then slowly moved into all-round defence, waiting for him to brief us on what was going on. A few moments later he was back with us, talking in a whisper. 'There's someone up ahead. Paddy and Kev, you stay here with the kit; Pete, drop your Bergen and come forward with me for a shufti.'

Without the heavy rucksack it was much easier to move quietly through the thick jungle, and it wasn't long before I could also hear something, or rather someone, a short distance in front of us. As we closed on the noise, I recognized the faint sound of somebody chopping wood. Lofty signalled to me to stop and slowly sank down into a position from where he could observe whatever it was that was in front of us. Frustratingly, I couldn't see a thing, but I knew better than to move. Lofty squatted down for several minutes then slowly made his way back to me.

'There's about a platoon's worth of Indonesians about forty

metres that way,' he told me, pointing through the foliage. 'They're not moving and a couple of them are cutting branches, but it's too early for them to be making camp so I don't know what they're doing. We'll head back to the others and make a detour.'

We made our way back to our RV with Kev and Paddy, backtracked a little, boxed around to the east then carried on, none the wiser as to what the Indos had been doing, but knowing, because we hadn't found their tracks, that they'd come from west of our route and that they might continue in the same direction and find our tracks instead.

We carried on through that day and the next, making slow but steady progress through the thick primary jungle, but then we began to hit the swamp that the other patrols had reported. It wasn't so bad at first, because round the edges it was only small pools with banks and raised mounds where it was possible to stay dry, but after a little while we started to get into deeper and deeper water, round our knees and some-times up to our waists.

The thing about this kind of swamp is that the jungle carries on beneath water level. You still have the same tangle of creepers, tree-roots, fallen branches and whatnot that you get on dry land, but all complicated by the fact that you can't see it. This means that progress is slower than ever, that you can't avoid making even more noise and commotion as you move and that you're very visible to any enemy watching the swamp. There's no question that this is really hard graft, physically and mentally, and the frustra-tion of staggering through the tangle of unseen obstructions can be increased by a feeling of powerlessness when you're a follower in the patrol rather than the leader. It can be difficult to remember that your main job at this point is scanning for the enemy and protecting the lead scout, but professionalism demands that you must. Mind you, the responsibility of leadership in this kind of situation isn't all beer and skittles either. Don told me that he developed this nasty suspicion that some Indonesian with a machine-gun was sitting there quietly laughing at us, waiting for him to get us into the perfect position to finish us off. Luckily for us he was wrong.

What was also worrying was that there was a fairly obvious 'high-tide' mark on the trees around where we were – and it was several metres above us! The danger wasn't so much from drowning, though that isn't impossible, but that in a heavy storm we might quickly find ourselves cut off by the water a long way behind enemy lines. It also meant that all kinds of jungle rubbish was sticking out of trees and bushes at a height where you wouldn't expect to see it, adding to the difficulty of moving.

We spent the next three days probing gently south trying to find a way through to the elusive river – and bloody knackering it was too! At one point, I'd gone with Don to check out a potential route, leaving Paddy and Kevin behind. As I waited twenty metres back from Don, watching him standing waist deep, pondering our next move, I suddenly had a flashback to the cowboy films we used to see at the pictures on a Saturday morning.

'Hey, Don,' I whispered, 'I hope we're the goodies.' He was lost in thought and it took him a few seconds to respond.

'What? What do you mean?' I shuffled over to where he was standing.

'I hope we're the goodies, because they always win. If we're the baddies, chances are we'll finish up with our hats floating on top of this lot.' Don started laughing, very quietly.

In all, we spent four days splashing around the swamp, trying to find a way through to the river. We knew we were close to our objective: sometimes we could hear diesel engines as launches ploughed up and down the open water. Once or twice, we even felt the wash of the boats going past.

When we actually found the river, it was almost an accident. We reached a low ridge of dry ground and made our way up onto it. From the top it opened up into what was obviously a disused and fairly overgrown rubber plantation, but through the more widely spaced trees we could see open water.

This took us into phase two of the operation. Our job now was to find a suitable position to establish an observation post that would allow us to watch the river without ourselves being visible from any angle. Don did a quick recce down to the riverbank and soon found a perfect position for us: a dried-up ditch surrounded by bushes, which offered a commanding view over a bend in the river, giving us the opportunity to see up- and downstream. The only danger of being observed was from a position back the way we had come; and that would only be when we took up our ambush positions. All in all, we were well set up.

We settled ourselves in and began the normal routine of watching and sleeping, waiting for some customers to turn up. We didn't have to wait long – the river was obviously a major thoroughfare – and there was evidently a military camp within a kilometre of us, given the number of transports that chugged past us. There were also a few fish-traps staked out in the water not far from us, and this was a little worrying because it was quite likely that someone would turn up to empty them from time to time. Despite this, Don was keen to make sure that we were ready for our 'bug-out' and, on his instructions, we brewed up tea every few hours, smoked, and made good hot meals each evening while we waited there. This was a far cry from the 'hard routine' that you learn during SAS jungle training but it actually worked: our morale was sky high; we were well fed and physically content; and we were fettled for the firefight and evasion that we knew was coming.

We spent four days sitting on the riverbank, watching oblivious Indonesians go past, reporting everything that moved on the river and waiting for the inevitable contact. The only really tense moment came when a couple of fishermen turned up to check the traps, unfortunately while Kevin was lurking close to the water's edge filling his water bottle. He was in decent cover but the bottle – on a length of paracord – was clearly visible to anyone looking in the right direction.

As it turned out, the two fishermen were concentrating too hard on the more important task of feeding their families to scope for enemy soldiers and their equipment, and they moved off without spotting him.

When Don decided that we'd been there long enough, he sent a signal back to Kuching requesting permission to move to our secondary task: the ambush. At this point there was a bit of a fumble. This was 1965 and the biggest thing in films was Sean Connery as James Bond. Lofty decided to cut short the usual cumbersome retasking request and got Paddy to send 'Request 00 licence'. In other words, a 'licence to kill'. Now this might seem a bit childish but, in reality, it was perfectly straightforward and comprehensible. Apart from sitreps and sighting reports, the only message that the Ops Room were expecting from us was one asking permission to mount our ambush and bug-out. Well, this was what we thought, and this was what everyone in the Ops Room thought as well. Everyone, that is, except the ops officer himself. Instead of a succinct 'yes' or 'no', what we got was a long-winded request for clarification, which meant wasted time as this was decoded and our reply encoded and sent off.

For patrols in the field, the farting about they did in the Ops Room could become a real pain in the arse. Operational security and integrity is very important to SAS-type operations, but you also have to be efficient, flexible and helpful with the troops on the ground, otherwise they lose confidence in you. One ops officer, who shall remain nameless, took operational security so seriously that he, quite rightly, never allowed anyone to see the operations map he maintained in his office in case it compromised the locations of patrols. Whenever anyone knocked on his door there was much elaborate folding and tucking of the heavy blue curtain that covered his map so that you never saw anything other than what you were supposed to see. All very well and good, until he took the map with him for a helicopter border recce, leaned out of the window to get a shufti and dropped the map, fully marked and on the wrong side of the border. Whoops-a-daisy!

In the end, though, clearance for the ambush came through and we began preparations for phase three.

The ambush was very simple. Lofty's plan was that he would take over the observation position whilst we waited in the OP (observation post). When a suitable target came along, he would initiate the ambush by opening fire and we would dash a couple of yards out of concealment and join in. As soon as the target was neutralized, we would make our way back into the jungle and extract back to a helicopter landing site on the border, which we should be able to reach the next day.

The next step was to pack our gear ready to leave. The ambush was going to be fairly easy – the Indos obviously had no idea we were there – but the problem lay with the getaway. During our approach to the river, we had come across several newly cut paths in the jungle that looked very much like rapid deployment lanes for the Indonesian base nearby. As soon as we shot up a boat on the river, the Indos were likely to come piling out of their camp in hot pursuit, and that was when things could turn nasty. Don set a time limit for our ambush: no later than an hour before dusk. If we hadn't got a target by then we would have to wait for the next day. This would give us the time to get out of the immediate area before darkness brought a halt to the Indo follow-up.

So there we sat, waiting for a target with tension steadily mounting. On the last four days there had been plenty of military traffic on the river for us to choose from, but on this one afternoon? Bugger all. Around 1500 hours it began to rain, gently at first but soon we could hear thunder in the distance, and we all began to wonder about our escape route. Would it still be there when the time came to bug-out?

But the sound of the rain had masked something else: the approach of a large motor launch. The first I knew about it was a hiss from Don, who was poised in an alert crouch just behind me. As we watched, this gleaming fifteen-metre boat slowly slid past us, flying the Indonesian flag and a number of military pennants, and we were all simply waiting for Lofty to squeeze off the first rounds and set the ball rolling. But he didn't.

Behind me I heard Kev muttering, 'What are we waiting for? The fucking *Ark Royal*?'

Lofty settled quietly down again. 'Sorry, lads, there were women on that boat. Might have been kids as well.'

There was no argument. No British soldier will willingly open fire on women and children, even if they are in a 'military target'.

We carried on waiting as the rain increased, lightning

flashed and thunder rolled around us. The intensity of a tropical downpour is difficult to explain to someone who hasn't
been in one: the noise is amazing; the crash of water pouring
through the jungle canopy and the hiss of rain hitting the
river drown out almost everything. We could have been
shouting to each other and no one on the river would have
heard us. As it was, I can now reveal that this was the first –
and possibly only – SAS ambush conducted with musical
accompaniment. Paddy had been doing something with the
radio and came across a music station broadcasting a dance
band. So he'd put the radio earpiece in a tin mug, which just
about amplified it enough for us all to hear it, and we were
happily listening to this as we waited for a target.

Just as we reached the deadline for that day, another
boat came into view. Another big one, but much more func-
tional in appearance, with a green canvas cover running
most of the length of it, and a built-in diesel engine. As it
passed us heading upstream, Don could see that its cargo
consisted of soldiers in green jungle fatigues and some
forty-gallon fuel containers. As it chugged out into
midstream, he gave the signal and all hell was immediately
let loose.

Lofty fired off the first shots, taking out two Indos sitting
at the back of the launch, and then we were all in position,
keeping up a steady rate of fire into the passenger area. In
those days, the 7.62mm SLR was still pretty much standard
in the Regiment, although there were couple of lighter, fully
automatic Armalites around for the squadron. Unfortunately,
one of these was in use by another patrol whilst the second
was being touted around as a piece of male jewellery by a
certain officer whose job at that time kept him well away
from the action. Even so, we weren't that bothered because
the big 7.62 rounds from our SLRs had awesome stopping

power: when you hit someone, you flattened them, and they could easily punch through several bodies, as well as a wooden bench or two, before they even began to slow down. Not surprisingly, no fire came back. In between the crashes of our rifles, all we could hear were the shouts and screams of the terrified Indos as our bullets tore through the flimsy boat.

Bugger! Sure enough, after firing four rounds my dodgy rifle got a stoppage. I knew it wasn't a gas problem because the regulator was set at zero but I didn't have time to set up an inquiry. Instead I had to cock it by hand after each round: not a big difficulty for someone who'd done his basic training with the old, bolt-actioned Lee-Enfield number 4 rifle, but a stupid situation nonetheless, and one that should never have happened.

Only a few seconds after Lofty fired the first round, it was all over. The noise of the ambush had temporarily frightened the jungle into silence, broken only by the hiss of rain on the river. No sound came from the boat as it drifted in the current, smoke pouring from beneath the canvas tarpaulin. As we changed magazines for the bug-out, a body rolled heavily into the water, then there was the *thud* of a fuel explosion from the rear of the boat.

Now it was time to move.

The drill was that Paddy and Kevin would pull back first, taking a position where they could cover me and Don as we scooted back through the rubber plantation to the comparative safety of the jungle. There was a slim chance that the ambush hadn't been heard because of the ferocity of the storm, but we couldn't count on it, and we had to accept that the Indo follow-up could be on us very quickly.

Kevin and Paddy were back in cover and now it was time for me and Don to get a shift on. We started running when, to my horror, Don did a fast about-turn and ran back towards the ambush position. My first thought was that we were cut off, but then I saw Don was getting his handy collapsible water-bag, which he'd left behind. He emptied it, rolled it up, and stuffed it down his shirt. He ran back past me saying, 'They ain't getting that!'

I'd nearly shat myself. 'Lofty, you bastard!'

We made good time bugging out from the ambush because the rain continued to crash down, which masked the sound of our movement. The only delay occurred when we came to the cut-off lane, which lay across our route back at the closest point to the Indo camp. Lofty, in the lead scout position, caught a sudden movement directly in front of him. I stopped and he carefully moved forward to the fallen tree where he'd seen the movement. As he got there, a great big cobra reared up at him, hissed then disappeared off into the undergrowth. He gave me the signal for 'snake', stepped over the log and carried on. I, in turn, passed the signal to Paddy who was behind me.

A little bit later, we stopped for a quick breather and Kev, the last man in the patrol, asked Don what the interruption had been. When Don told him, he went ballistic. Paddy hadn't passed on the message and Kev had a bit of a thing about snakes. 'You fuckin' Irish bastard! I might've been scoffed.'

Kevin hated snakes. On one long operation we were due to be resupplied by airdrop but, through simple bad luck, the resupply bundle with all our fresh rations got hooked up in the trees. This left us with a problem because we were going to have to attempt to survive off the jungle for several days whilst still attempting to fulfil our task: no easy job. Even worse, the mail package contained a thirty-pound tax refund I was due! In the end we went down to a local kampong where we knew the aboriginals. They looked after us very well and we joined them in a big cook-up in their longhouse that evening. One dish was a spicy meat stew, which tasted great, and we all got heavily stuck in, particularly Kevin. At the end of the evening we asked what it had been made from. The answer? Python.

Just before last light, well pleased with our progress, we looped off our route and back-ambushed the way we'd come. As we lay amongst some fallen trees we heard the *whoosh!* of mortar bombs being launched. Mortars are terrifying in the jungle because the bombs usually explode when they hit the canopy, rather than the ground, creating an effect like an airburst and showering a much wider area with lethal shrapnel. Fortunately, we could hear that the explosions were some way off and Kev, who'd been a mortar instructor in the Paras, said, 'We're OK, they're firing to the east.'

I felt relieved at this news, but this was punctured by Don, the veteran of Korea and Malaya. 'Why do you think they're not firing here?' The answer was obvious: because this was where their troops were looking for us.

'Shit!'

Despite this, Don told us to get a brew on and a good meal inside us ready for the next day, and we got our heads down for the night, safe enough because only an idiot will try to patrol in the jungle at night.

Next morning we were up before first light and ready for the off. We made good time and soon got into primary jungle – relatively easy going because there's very little undergrowth beneath the thick canopy – and by mid-afternoon we were within striking distance of the border. Now things began to get more complicated. Paddy was beginning to feel the effects of his appendix operation and was dehydrating fast, but we had to assume that the Indonesian follow-up was fairly close behind us.

The choice that faced Don was whether to push on, staying ahead of the follow-up but risking Paddy getting into a bad way, or to stop and call for a helicopter to lift us out, but risking the Indos catching up while we waited. He called a quick 'Chinese parliament' and we went for the second option.

Against the odds, Don's request was granted almost immediately, and shortly afterwards, after we'd gone a little further, an RAF chopper appeared, hovering over the trees directly to our front. Don switched on his SARBE and a few moments later the helicopter was directly over us.

We had no voice communication in those days, so we couldn't talk to the crew, but they dropped a can with a message to say they were going to winch us up. Don told me to go first, but because of the height of the trees the winch line couldn't reach us, so the crewman attached some parachute strap, making a large loop in place of the usual two slings. The winch was lowered, the two slings rotating slowly. Don put the four rucksacks on one sling and I got into the other. This was a bit dicey, as the pilot had to juggle with the helicopter to clear me of the trees, and as he did so, the rucksacks fell off. It could just as easily have been me.

The helicopter carried me the two hundred metres or so to our LZ and lowered me down to be met by the platoon who'd escorted us over the border in the first place. As my feet touched the ground and I unhooked myself from the strap, their company sergeant major handed me a mug of tea, which was very nice of him, and the chopper roared off to pick up the rest of the lads.

It wasn't too long before we were back in Kuching and headed for the Ops Room for a debrief. After we'd cleaned our weapons and had handed them in to the armoury, I grabbed a yard or so of flannelette, the cloth strip we pulled through our rifle barrels and, after a whispered briefing, got the rest of the lads to tie them round their arms. We went through the whole patrol in detail with the ops officer, the intelligence collator and 'Punchy' Williams, the new OC who'd just taken over from Roger Woodiwiss. Once we'd finished what we had to say, and got up to head off for some scoff, Punchy stopped us.

'I don't want to sound stupid, but why are you wearing white armbands?'

'Sorry, sir, we forgot to take them off. It's the reason we've got away with it so long. We've been dressing as umpires.'

It's a tradition that at the end of every operational tour, we hold a party to thank everyone who has helped us and to let off as much steam as possible before we head for home (we also have one when we get home for the wives and families, to thank them for their support), and this occasion was no different. Of course, it's also a chance for the squadron naughty boys to get up to some spectacularly bad behaviour and we were rarely disappointed in that either. This time, the early part of the festivities was enlivened by Kevin, who'd got himself so pissed that Bob Turnbull had had him tied to a fence near where some Kiwi SAS lads had a pig tethered for that night's barbecue. Mostly this was to prevent him injuring himself, of course, but there was some speculation about the possibility of mistaken identity when it came to killing the pig.

The chief guest was the brigade commander who turned up with his wife and teenage daughter, all looking very spruce in their civvy finery. Despite Punchy Williams' and Bob Turnbull's efforts, he inevitably managed to spot Kevin who was effing and blinding at the top of his voice: 'Fuckin' let me go, you Kiwi bastards!'

They moved on to the immaculately manicured lawn and the hierarchy began making polite small talk, with Punchy making use of his most *refained* accent. Now we had a sort of love-hate relationship with Punchy, who'd previously been the adjutant and who was, in SAS terms, a big fat pest. When the party kicked off, I was just as pissed as Kevin was, though I'd been somewhat more successful at staying out of trouble, but it hadn't taken much for two of the other lads, Ken Connor and Dick Tubman, to persuade me that it would be a good idea to empty one of the fire buckets over Punchy when they gave the signal. Consequently, I was lurking round one corner of the house whilst Punchy, the brigadier and company made their way slowly towards me.

They were just round the corner when Ken gave the thumbs down and I stepped out and let fly with the bucket. Whoops! I missed Punchy but got the brigadier's daughter, who was now covered in a rather unpleasant mixture of water, piss, spit, dog-ends, dead insects and all the other detritus that collects in the fire buckets at SAS parties. Punchy forced a grin as I ducked away: 'Oh dear, I am sorry. It looks like the lads are getting a little boisterous. If you'll excuse me, I'll just go and see what's happening.'

Still grinning stupidly, he edged towards the corner and then nipped round it, breaking into full speed (not too fast in his case, the fat git) as he spotted me haring off. The accent slipped a bit as he chased after me.

'Come back here, Scholey, you cunt! I'll fucking RTU you when I catch you, you bastard!'

He didn't have a hope, and soon made his way back to the party where the brigadier's daughter had now been more or less cleaned up.

'I'm so sorry, Brigadier, they're good boys really but they do get a little exuberant . . .' he told them, laughing weakly.

By now, I was on the balcony with the second bucket, lurking just above him. Dick Tubman gave the signal again and I let go with the second bucket: a direct hit! Punchy momentarily forgot himself: 'Scholey, you fuckin' arsehole! . . . Oh sorry, Brigadier!'

The party carried on as we all got drunker and drunker, the Brigadier and his family watching with fixed grins as we did the 'Dance of the Zulu Warrior' as a kind of prelude to the *hangi*.* After we'd eaten, some of the boys decided that we should start ripping each other's shirts off. I was standing watching when Taff Brown, who was one of the squadron's slightly more pukka members, crept up behind me and tore off my shirt, ripping away all the buttons with a roar of drunken laughter. I was sober enough to remember that he had about ten more shirts hanging in his locker upstairs, so I went and got one of those and put it on. Sure enough, ten minutes later, Taff had torn this off as well. I repeated the procedure and so did he, getting through six of his shirts in the process. Then someone tore his shirt off and he went up to get another.

All in all, I spent the best part of that party on the run.

Being back home gave me the chance to get to know Hereford a little better and to resume some of my hobbies, which in those days centred around beer-drinking, betting on the horses and the better class of young lady living in the Hereford area.

It was around now that I met my future wife Carolyn. Thinking to demonstrate my more sensitive side, I took her

* *Hangi*: pig-roast.

to see *Snow White and the Seven Dwarfs*. Everything was going smoothly until Grumpy appeared.

'Look, it's Kevin,' I exclaimed, struck by the uncanny resemblance.

'Shut up, Scholey,' an indignant voice bellowed from the darkness.

The audience, composed mostly of SAS members it seemed, erupted.

Soon after this incident, we got a long weekend's leave and I invited Kevin to come back to Brighton with me. I had a longer time off than Kev, who had to be back on the Monday whilst I had until Thursday morning but, nothing daunted, we went out for a few beers on Sunday evening, and eventually rolled back at about four thirty on Monday morning.

Kev got his head down for a couple of hours and at ten to eight, I woke him, we got dressed and had a cup of tea. Then I took him down to Brighton station about twenty minutes' walk away.

By the time we arrived at the station it was twenty-five past eight and Kev's train was due to leave at 0830. He heard an announcement over the tannoy, rushed to his platform and leaped on the train just as it was pulling out. Meanwhile, I headed for home.

At about eleven o'clock there was a ring at the doorbell: Kevin.

'What happened?' I asked.

'I'm in the shit now. They'll post me AWOL.'

'But what happened?'

'It wasn't the right train. As it pulled out, I realized there was no one else on it. It went four hundred yards up the line and stopped. Then these big brushes started to wash the bloody thing down. I sat in that train for an hour before it moved back to the station.'

I went into the other room to laugh. He phoned the Regiment and fortunately everything was okay, except of course that everyone knew about it in seconds.

My second tour of Borneo, which kicked off in June 1967, was an entirely different kettle of fish. By then, an outbreak of peace was in the offing. Sukarno was gone, replaced by General Suharto in a bloody coup, while the pragmatists of the Indonesian military were in the ascendancy and keen to bring the confrontation to as quick an end as possible, without giving the impression that they'd had their arses kicked – which, of course, they had. In previous months, entire infantry companies, and even complete SAS squadrons, had been crossing the border to hit Indonesian targets and the Indos had lost their stomach for the fight completely.

Which meant that when we arrived there wasn't all that much to do. We sent out patrols to monitor the border but we stayed on our side and, in reality, they were training as much as operations. We also did a fair bit of straightforward training as well, and before too long, when negotiations had reached a crucial stage, we were sent away from mainland Borneo, as a goodwill gesture to the Indos, to the island of Santubong down the river and off the coast of Sarawak.

Santubong was a beautiful place: a small island with a white sandy beach and a bit of jungle. We were given a pile of fresh rations and, for some strange reason, a vast quantity of Merrydown cider. We travelled there in a small flotilla of flat-bottomed assault boats and, once we'd got our tents set up, we named it 'Merrydown Camp'.

But, being the SAS, we couldn't just have a straightforward holiday could we? No, we had to do some training, or at least pretend to, to justify our lotus eating existence. Fortunately, nobody took this too seriously.

First up it was decided that Willie Mundell would teach us how to do assault landings. So I and a few others from 18 Troop were detailed off to have first go while the rest of the lads got on with their sunbathing and swimming. We set off out to sea for a kilometre or so, turned round and then came screaming in towards the beach with the two forty-horse-power engines going at full tilt. In theory, the next move would be to cut the engines at a certain distance from the beach then sweep in all silent and deadly.

Anyway, Alfie Tasker was at the controls and when Willie gave him the signal . . . er, nothing happened. The engines continued to roar and we were still skewering towards the beach at high speed. By now we were in a bit of a panic. Taff Springles was standing in the front, waving his shirt to try to warn the swimmers, and we could see Clancy Bean splashing about in front of us, desperately trying to get out of the way. Fortunately, we shot past everyone in the water and now the only obstacle was the beach. Alfie was still trying to cut the engines but nothing doing, and we piled in at high speed. I was standing near the front and as we hit, I was heaved out into the surf. As I got up, undamaged, I looked round to see the boat half way out of the water with the engines still churning away like mad, and Alfie Tasker jumping out onto what he thought was the beach and disappearing under the water.

So that was the end of beach landings. Next came fishing.

Ray Allen, a big Yorkshire lad, fixed up an ammunition box full of plastic explosive and he, Alan Lonney and a couple of others took the boat out to where they thought the fish were. First they dropped Ray on a little island and then couldn't get him off because the tide had gone out; then an hour or so later when they had retrieved him, they took the great bomb out to where they thought the fish were, lit the blue touch-paper, dropped it in . . . and stalled the boat. They calmly tried to get it going again, then they panick- ingly tried to start it up, then one of them dived over the side and started swimming. With a few seconds to go, the engine started and the boat almost stood on its tail as they pulled away from the danger zone, slowing down to pick up the swimmer. Alas, it was too late. With a huge roar the depth charge went off and a vast column of water rose up and flipped them all into the sea. They all swam back to the beach clutching on to the upturned boat. No fish were caught.

So no more fishing. Time for water-skiing.

Willie said, 'Who fancies a drag on the planks?' and I thought, Yeah, why not? So I got the kit on and zoomed out about a mile or so, then I fell off. I wasn't the world's greatest swimmer then and as I was splashing about in the water, I realized I couldn't feel the bottom. This started me thinking, What if there's sharks?

Anyway, Brummie Hassall saw me floundering around and started swimming out to me, and he'd been going about fifteen minutes when he got cramp so the boat, which by now was coming to get me, had to stop to pick him up and take him back to the beach so they could massage his legs and get him going again. Meanwhile, I'd now got myself close enough to the beach that I could put my feet on the sand and I was able to walk in.

Next up was Pickett, who got in the boat, started it up, then fell out and wound up with the boat circling round and round him like some demented shark. And he was followed by Nick who started the boat up, but got the propeller stuck in the sand. When he went to free it he managed to lacerate the insides of his thighs. This probably wasn't as bad as it looked but led the five assembled patrol medics to start fighting over who got to suture him. Nick was followed by the cook, who managed exactly the same thing.

The only option now was to start drinking heavily. We settled down with some Merrydown and I spent the next hour or so doing my 'turn', taking the piss out of each member of the squadron in turn. Then there was a dull thud.

'What was that?'

'The camp's on fire.'

Someone had chucked a cigarette end into the shit-pit and ignited it all. We rushed around like headless chickens for a few minutes before someone got a big tarpaulin and threw it over the burning crapper. That put it out and we carried on. Then Ron Barker went out to see if it was okay, lifted the tarpaulin and it went up again.

'Leave it alone, Barker, you twat!'

Then someone said, 'Let's get the Army Air Corps up here for a party!' Someone got on the radio and gave them a call and an hour or so later, three or four choppers turned up with all these Army Air Corps lads on board, come to spend the night with us. We were all very friendly, giving it loads of glad-handing and smiles until, around half past one, a big fight broke out: SAS versus AAC. We all got stuck in and gave them a good thumping.

Next morning we all got up with our black eyes and thick lips, and helped the Air Corps boys into their choppers: 'Great party, lads, thanks . . .'

Finally it was time to return to Kuching in the two assault boats. We had a bit of a problem now because the shear-pins from the engines kept breaking and we only had one left. This meant that one boat would have to tow the other all the way back down the river. As we were loading the boats, Alfie Tasker handed me the pin. I dropped it, and watched with my heart in my mouth, as it spiralled out of sight into the blue water. Oh, shit.

Alfie Tasker grabbed the front of my shirt. 'Scholey, when we get back, you are fucking dead. You understand that, don't you?'

Two hours of hard rowing later, we were back in Kuching only to find that Captain Mackay-Lewis was missing. He'd taken Punchy's little sailing boat upriver and somehow managed to get lost. He showed up eight or nine hours later, sunburned and dishevelled. We weren't impressed.

'Typical fucking officer. How can you get lost on a river? You go up it, then all you've got to do is come back down again.'

A few days later, we flew out, heading for Singapore. We were in an RAF Britannia, I think, and I wound up sitting near the front. We were bored and tired, but for some reason, I couldn't sleep. I'd read everything on the aircraft, including the emergency card, about four times. By now the cabin lights were dimmed and everyone had more or less settled down.

But I was still restless (the lads used to say I walked to our destinations, moving up and down the cabin) and as I sat there, twitching away, I bent over and pulled a life-jacket out from under my seat. I tried it on and found that it fitted rather well, so I sat there in the life-jacket with a can of soft drink left over from my 'haversack rations'.

After a few minutes of this, the life-jacket was getting a little sweaty and I decided to take it off. But on the cramped aircraft, this meant standing up. I did this and was wrestling my way out of the rubbery yellow embrace of my RAF 'Mae West' when some of my drink splashed on the regimental second-in-command who was asleep in the row of seats behind me. This woke him up, and his first sight was Scholey, stood there with his life-jacket on.

'Bloody hell, Scholey! What on earth's happening?'

I couldn't resist it. 'Sir, we're ditching in about thirty seconds!'

This took a couple of seconds to sink in.

'Fucking hell!'

There was about five minutes of complete panic as the flower of the Special Air Service struggled into their life-jackets, followed by a period of anger and sullen resentment as revenge was plotted. My reward was a £20 fine, two weeks extra duties and an involuntary dunking in the standing water reservoir at Changi Field, Singapore. Oh, well. I did think, though: Scream and shout in a library, and everyone thinks you're a loony, but do it in a plane and they all join in.

The stop off in Singapore gave us a chance to unwind a bit more, as well as allowing the Malayan lags to revisit their old haunts. One visit we made was to an ordnance depot where Kevin spotted a big pile of interesting-looking boots.

' 'Ere, what are those, mate?'

'They are experimental jungle boots.'

We looked at these boots which were a sensible concoction of canvas, leather and rubber, apparently ideally suited to our purposes.

'Do you mind if we blag a few pairs then, matey?'

'Sorry, pal, I'd love to help but those have got to be destroyed.'

It turned out that these boots had failed the trial and no amount of pleading, even with Lofty adding his weight, could get them to give them to us, even though they looked, at least, as though they were ideally suited to our needs. Our problem was that the army issue jungle boots, which in those days were knee-high canvas and rubber lace-ups, used to fall apart after a couple of weeks' hard use, which effectively meant that we were getting through two or three pairs on every patrol. Standard army ankle boots were really too heavy for jungle use, so we wound up using a range of civvy boots, or modifying the issue ones, which was a pain the arse. In fact we didn't resolve the problem until we were given the excellent US issue boots a few years later.

We had a few days in Singapore and naturally decided to have a bit of a drink one evening in the transit accommodation we were occupying. After a couple of bottles of Tiger, we began to run short of booze until somebody spotted Kevin's duty frees lying on his bed. A single man at this stage, Kevin hadn't bothered to waste any money on scent or anything poncy like that, but instead had opted for six bottles of vodka, reasoning that the import duty wouldn't be too severe. It didn't take us long to get through it but we were sober enough at the end to top up the bottles with water.

Somehow I'd imagined that he wouldn't spot the switch until after we'd got back to camp, but I suppose that going through customs and having to fork out several quid in import duty had reminded him that he was carrying dangerous cargo. Anyway, he opened a bottle in the coach just after we left Lyneham. It's hard to imagine the shock he must have received, taking a swig of what he thought was going to be export strength vodka and finding it was Singaporean tap water.

'FUCKING HELL! YOU FUCKING BASTARDS!'

Just south of Hereford, on the A49 Ross Road, there's a hill called the Callow. As you come over the top of it you can see Hereford in front of you, and Dinedor hill off to the left. In those days in the sixties, when we were alternating between tough operational tours, where our lads were being killed

116

and wounded, every time we came back over the Callow, the bus broke out in cheers. We'd made it; we'd survived; and, above all, we were home.

The Scholey family at home – wife Carolyn, daughter Amy and son David who gave me their unwavering support at all times.

My mother Violet, taken outside our home in Brighton during the war. She brought up six of us while my father was serving in the RAF.

My dad George, taken in the 1950s. He never missed a chance to 'perform', a trait he passed on to me.

My grandad George Stephen Haslen, with his dog Biddy. He served in both the Boer and First World Wars.

Just after passing out parade in the Royal Regiment of Artillery 1957. Gunner Scholey is on the far right.

3 Platoon, A Company, Paras. Two sticks of fifteen waiting at RAF Akrotiri, Cyprus to board Hastings aircraft for an exercise in Libya, early 1960s.

Sgt Major Andy Morrison briefing A Company before our quick move to Kuwait, which was threatened with invasion by Iraq, 1961.

A Company disembarking from Royal Marines landing craft after a day's intensive training in beach assaults, Kuwait 1961.

Heavy drop of Land Rover and trailer using three 60-foot diameter parachutes which cut away on impact. Paras de-rig it ready to drive away.

Kevin Walsh (right) seen here with his pal in 1 Para. Later we were to serve together on many ops with 18 Troop.

A Squadron inside a Belvedere helicopter. First left is John 'Lofty' Wiseman, author of *The SAS Survival Handbook*.

D Squadron 1964. Front row, on attachment, Capt Akehurst and Sgt Major Konor, US Special Forces.

BORNEO CAMPAIGN – D SQUADRON TOUR 1965

Myself and patrol with local border scouts (used as jungle trackers) awaiting resupply by helicopter. Landing zone secured by other personnel.

Taken by Lofty (patrol commander) en route to a forward base for infiltration in to enemy territory on fourteen day operation.

17 Troop test-firing weapons ready for ops the following day. Nothing is left to chance.

Landing zone secure, patrol wait for lift-out.

Base signallers being moved to a forward base.

Myself with Tony Ball and Pete Hogg enjoying three days R&R in Kuching.

The parachuting monkey, nick-named 'Scholey'– cheek! After seven jumps he was appointed freefall troop mascot.

ADEN CAMPAIGN – D SQUADRON

18 Troop await heli-lift to support 16 Troop who are engaged in firefight with enemy.

Five-minute breather en route to secure the high ground in Radfan mountains while Royal Marines do low ground sweep to flush out enemy.

18 Troop preparing to move to intercept enemy who are advancing to attack forward base. 16, 17 and 19 Troops already en route – no problem!

PARACHUTING WITH 16 TROOP, D SQUADRON

16 Troop D Squadron at the Norwegian Army Parachute School, Trondheim, late 1960s.

Myself and 'Spider' Martin at Trondheim.

3 Platoon A Company on the Jebel Akhdar, northern Oman, early 1960s.

My turn for three days R&R in Salalah after eight weeks ops on the Jebel. Now in B Squadron on our first tour with G Squadron in the Regiment's 'secret war' in Dhofar, southern Oman.

Baroness Thatcher (then Prime Minister) on a visit to the Regiment in the early 1980s.

Iranian Embassy Siege, 1980. B Squadron assault the rear of the building

The soldier without his hood is Tommy Palmer. He was forced to rip it of when it caught fire, but he pressed on with the attack while inhaling gas and smoke. For this he was rightly awarded the Queen's Gallantry Medal.

HRH the Prince of Wales after a live firing demonstration by the anti-terrorist team. He was somewhat bemused by the fury and aggression of the experience, though he seemed to enjoy it. Seen here with Major General Sir Michael Rose, then the C.O. of the Regiment.

My wife Carolyn and myself chat with Prince Charles during an informal visit to the Sergeants' Mess, December 1981.

CHAPTER FIVE

My first trip out to Aden with the SAS came a little while after I'd joined the D Squadron Mobility Troop. We'd gone out there for a training exercise, getting to know the Pink Panthers, getting to know desert conditions and practising cooperation with the RAF, but although there was a certain amount of tension in the area at the time and A Squadron had lost a couple of guys in a kick-up in the Radfan mountains, we weren't out there to start mixing it.

Even so, it was tough going. I was the new boy in the troop, so I was on a steep learning curve and trying to keep up with all the information being fired at me by the old lags as I was assimilated into the troop and the squadron. Of course, I wasn't a new boy in Arabia – I'd seen operations in Kuwait and garrison duties in Bahrain when I was with 2 Para – but now I was SAS and it was all change.

We'd no more dipped our toe into Aden than we were back in Hereford and preparing for the squadron deployment to Borneo, which of course meant getting our minds round the concepts and techniques essential for jungle warfare and putting the desert stuff on the back-burner.

Even so, events in Aden were clearly building up a head

119

of steam and it didn't take the brains of an archbishop to understand that there was every likelihood of us becoming further involved. Oddly enough, though, it wasn't until 1966 that D Squadron got there in an operational capacity whilst the problems had actually started years before. In fact things had been pretty uncomfortable for the British in the Middle East for a long time, going back even to the First World War and Lawrence of Arabia. Way back then, most of the Middle East, Arabia and the Persian Gulf had been ruled by the Ottoman Empire from Turkey. But Turkey had been coming apart at the seams for years and the First World War – Turkey joined in on Germany's side – changed everything. In 1916, with British help, the Arabs, led by King Hussein of Jordan's great-grandfather, had revolted against the Turks and begun the process of pushing them out of the Arabian peninsula. This was where Lawrence of Arabia came in: he was military adviser to one of the main Arab commanders and led the Arab army when they captured the key objectives of Aqabah, the port at the top of the Red Sea, and Damascus.

When the war came to an end, though, the Arabs didn't get half of what we'd promised them at the start of the revolt. Instead, the usual series of dirty deals was played out, and a good chunk of the Middle East was carved up between Britain and France. So – surprise, surprise – it was hard to find a huge number of Arabs with anything nice to say about us.

Britain stuck it out through the twenties and thirties, with garrisons in Egypt, Palestine, Aden, Iraq and in some of the Gulf States: but even back then these states were trouble-some, and after the Second World War, when Britain was on its uppers, the writing was on the wall and we had to start to pull out.

So by the beginning of the 1960s, everything had pretty much changed. We had a garrison in Bahrain on the Persian Gulf, a garrison in Aden at the southern end of the Arabian peninsula, which was well positioned for stop-offs for aircraft and ships going further east to Hong Kong and Singapore, as well as a scattering of airbases in friendly countries like Oman, where there was often a small British presence in the form of advisers and so on. Aden, which was the location for the Headquarters British Forces Middle East, was a strange enough place. The port and city – which was bustling and cosmopolitan – had been under British control for more than a hundred years because of its role as a staging post for India and the Far East, but the interior of the country, sometimes called south Yemen, was very different. Partly desert and partly mountain, real power was in the hands of tribal chiefs and minor warlords, who were paid by the British to keep their areas in order. If the cash was late, or they were feeling stroppy, they kicked up a fuss; otherwise, they were our best mates.

By and large this policy had worked until the early sixties but with General Nasser making a row in Egypt, and with our old mates from the KGB active in the area, it was only a matter of time before something went wrong. As it turned out, this was a coup by the army in Yemen, which got rid of the hereditary Imam and set up the usual left-wing government instead. Soon after, with Egyptian and Soviet backing, they started moving arms and guerrillas over the Radfan mountains into Adeni territory.

Nobody took a lot of notice of this at first. I don't suppose anyone really knew it was happening, and by the time they did, it had really taken hold. Grenades were being thrown about, district officers were being shot at and everything had turned totally pear-shaped. A state of emergency was declared at the end of 1963 and shortly after that the UK government announced that they were planning to give Aden independence, though keeping hold of the British bases.

This was meant to pacify the rebels, but it had no real effect, so the next big plan was to use military force. We'd put together a small colonial army in Aden, the Federal Regular Army (or FRA), and they cobbled together a task force and sent it up into the hills. Seeing this lot coming, the rebels hightailed it for the safety of the Yemen and all went quiet.

Unfortunately, having occupied their positions in the mountains, the FRA didn't have much idea of what they were supposed to do next. They didn't collect any intelligence, they didn't do any 'hearts and minds' work and they didn't catch any baddies. When they eventually sloped off to their barracks, the rebels came straight back over the border.

After this first cock-up it was time for a second approach. The headshed in Aden had a rethink and decided that they would use British forces as well as the FRA, and this, by a complicated string of coincidences, was how the SAS got involved.

At this time in 1964, the officer commanding A Squadron was Peter de la Billière (known generally as DLB – which is short for 'Dead Letter Box' – or to me as 'ta-ra-ra boom-de-ay', a nickname that, strangely, hadn't much amused him). He'd previously had a staff job in Aden and when the Radfan operation was being set up happened to be out there setting up a training exercise for A Squadron. The plan involved using two battalions of the FRA together with 45 Commando Royal Marines (with B Company of 3 Para, then based in Bahrain, attached to them) to secure two hill objectives in rebel-held areas, one of which would be taken in an airborne assault by the Paras. DLB thought that his lads might be used to secure the Paras' DZ (Drop Zone).

By all accounts it was rather a rushed job. A Squadron arrived in Aden in April 1964 and after a couple of days moved up to a forward base in the mountains. Then they set about patrolling to get the lie of the land and acclimatize themselves to the harsh conditions. This meant trying to operate in extreme heat – it could easily reach 120° Fahrenheit during the day – with just the water you could carry: a couple of two pint bottles on your belt, maybe, and another container in your Bergen. This, of course, restricted the scope of the operations they could mount.

After less than a week of patrolling, DLB was given orders for his main operation: sending an eight man patrol to secure 3 Para's DZ at the head of the Wadi Taym, which was well inside rebel-held territory. They were going to lie up for a period, observing enemy activity, before emerging to clear and mark their target.

The operation started at last light on 29 April 1963 with a heli drop-off of the patrol 5000 metres inside rebel-held territory. They began to move forwards towards their LUP (lying up point) when they hit their first problem: Nick Warburton, the patrol signaller, fell ill with suspected food poisoning. Although he managed to keep going, he slowed the patrol down and it became evident that they couldn't reach their objective before daybreak.

This meant that they were up shit creek without a paddle in sight. If they were spotted, it was likely that they would be outnumbered and quite possibly overwhelmed by the rebels – referred to by the press as the 'Red Wolves' – who were known to be in the area. They were well out of range of artillery support and probably not strong enough to secure an LZ for helicopter extraction: all in all, a poor situation to find themselves in. After a quick Chinese parliament, they decided to try to find an emergency lie-up and wait it out.

Disaster struck during the late morning when an armed man wandered up to where they were hiding. Almost inevitably he saw them and did a runner, and with a split second to make the decision, Geordie shot him.

The killing of the man started an immediate reaction from the locals who, not surprisingly, were keen to find out what was going on in their area. As they approached, a firefight developed and the patrol was soon trapped by an increasing number of angry rebels. For the rest of the day there was a stalemate. Once the shooting had started the patrol had called for air support and there was a steady shuttle of RAF jets coming in to strafe and rocket the guerrillas, but the rebels' firepower was sufficient to keep the SAS pinned down.

Darkness meant the end of close air support but it also gave the patrol the opportunity to make a break for it. By now the enemy snipers were closing on the SAS position, and as the patrol prepared to move, Warburton, the signaller, was shot in the head and killed. A few minutes later, as they left their shelter, the patrol commander, a young captain called Robin Edwards, was also killed.

Leaving the two bodies, the patrol skirmished towards a wadi that would cover their retreat to safety. During the remainder of the night, they fought their way back along the wadi, occasionally 'back-ambushing' their track to deter follow-up by the rebels. By morning, the survivors were safely back in friendly territory. So, not a great start to operations in Aden, but at least it forced the rest of us to remember that it wasn't going to be easy.

But before we went out to Aden, we found ourselves getting a bit of a warm-up in Libya, of all places. In fact, before Colonel Gaddaffi took power in 1969, British troops exercised there quite regularly, going over a lot of the same ground that had been fought over during the Second World

War when the SAS had first been formed. The idea of this particular deployment was to test the Pinkies in true desert conditions, and to get us all up to speed with desert navigation, astral navigation and so on.

One interesting aspect of this exercise was the army's attempt to teach us how to ride camels (better than smoking them). I can't quite remember why – maybe it was one of Lofty's gags – but Kevin was selected to go off with a couple of Arabs to learn the basics so that he could then impart his new-found skills to the rest of us. It was coming up to noon, the hottest time of day in the desert, and it was a tad warm at about 130° Fahrenheit in the shade as we all lined up to watch the demo.

By now Kevin and the camel had decided that they really didn't like each other. Every time he tried to get it to do something it didn't want to, it spat on him, and each gob of camel spit was about the size of a lumpy, stinking dinner plate. After ten minutes of argy-bargy, the camel finally hauled itself to its feet, nearly catapulting Kev off as it rose. Now, following the instructions of his Arab teachers, he walloped it on the arse with a cane. This should have put it into a steady jog-trot but instead the camel bolted, accelerating to about 30 m.p.h. as Kev clung on for dear life. It got about five kilometres into the wilderness before slumping down and refusing to move. Kevin came up on the walkie-talkie to ask the Arab how to get it moving again. The response was none too helpful. 'I don't know. It's never done that before.'

An hour went by as we watched the distant black blob through our binoculars, desperately trying to get the camel back 'on the road'. Poor Kevin was in a bit of a state by now, having left his water-bottle behind, and occasionally came up on the walkie-talkie effing and blinding about this and that: camels, Arabs and the army mostly. Then, suddenly, we saw the camel set off again at high speed in our direction, dragging Kevin behind it. Not long afterwards, he returned, knackered, battered and thirsty.

'Hello, Kev, back with us?'

'I am never going on a fuckin' camel again. Anyone who wants me to can fuck off!'

'How did you get it moving?'

'The bastard. I shouted at it, pleaded with it . . . in the end I stuck a hexi-block under it and lit it, that got the fucker going!'

Which was the last time we experimented with camels on that trip.

Much of the training in Libya involved driving out into the sand sea, navigating from point to point, and learning the technique for keeping the vehicles from bogging into the sand. Experience showed us that the areas around the top of the dunes tended to be very soft and if we weren't going fast enough, we would almost inevitably bog in up to the axles, whereas a fast approach gave us enough momentum to get over the top and start down the other side. This usually worked except, of course, for the one occasion when the crest of the dune turned out to be rock-hard and the Pinkie took off like Evel Knievel. So far so good, but then the tail hit the sand on the way down and damn nearly flipped the whole thing through 180 degrees. Kev was thrown forwards and would have fallen over the front had Lofty not grabbed him by his belt and pulled him in. We reached the bottom and Paddy slammed on the brakes, at which point Kevin really did get flung out, landing in a small cursing heap on the sand in front of us. Lofty and I got out to check that the vehicle was OK and the next thing we saw was Kevin and Paddy, locked together as they attempted to batter the living crap out of each other, rolling the remainder of the way down the sand dune. By the time they reached the bottom, they were so knackered they'd decided to call it a draw and they returned to the Rover with no harm done. We paused for a brew to calm down and then Lofty announced, 'Right, I'll drive. Pete, you sit in the front; you two can stay in the back,' and off we went again.

Lofty wanted to prove a point now. He started up, got the Rover in gear and set it off at the next dune, foot hard down. As we hit the crest, I decided enough was enough: I bailed out the side and jogged down the dune as Lofty took the heavy Rover through a terrifying slide towards the bottom.

'What are you doing, Pete? Get back in, you fucking coward!'

I couldn't disagree with him, but I can't help noticing from my military service that there are a lot of dead heroes in cemeteries around the world, and a lot of live cowards sitting in front of the television with their slippers on and a cup of tea at their elbow, looking at their pension statements. It's worth thinking about.

Once we'd finished in the sand sea we returned to a slightly more solid area where we worked closely with a squadron of RAF Hunters out of El Adem airfield. This was to give us practice in avoiding fighter ground-attack and added up to fairly useful training: whenever aircraft noise was heard, we went through various drills to disperse the troop, as well as slinging high-priority equipment off the vehicles so that if they got hit, the key stores and equipment would survive. (It was perfectly logical when you think about it – the Pinkies were the biggest targets.) The Hunters took gun camera film rather than actually shooting, and these were passed on to us so that we could make our own tactical appreciations.

Normally we stopped at midday when it became too hot to

train, but we would always take a shot of the sun to determine our position and then laager up (as opposed to lagering-up, which we generally did after operations), positioning the vehicles facing outwards for easy dispersal. When it had cooled, we would continue, making our way from RV to RV, relying on astral navigation to fix our position.

When evening came the temperature was quite pleasant and at night it was actually icy. This brought on a problem that Kevin was having with his back. He'd injured it parachuting some time before and his various exploits with camels and Rovers had made it worse, so much so that he was having difficulty sleeping. One morning, Don asked me if I could give him something to help him. I broke out the medical pack, pulled out a bottle of tablets and passed four to Kev.

'Here you go, mate, get these down your neck.'

He shovelled the tablets into his mouth and as I put the bottle back in the medical kit I glanced at the label. Bollocks!

'Kev, spit 'em out *now*!'

'Why?'

'Because you'll be dead in an hour if you don't.' He would have been too. I'd given him the wrong pills.

'You fucking prat, Scholey!'

He spat them out and I gave him two different ones, which he swallowed.

'What were those, then, Scholey?'

'Piriton.'

'What are they for?' he asked suspiciously.

'Bites and stings,' I said, tongue-in-cheek.

'What the fuck do I want those for?'

'Lofty said your back's been bit.'

'You arsehole, he said my back's in shit.'

'Well,' I said jokingly, 'you might have swallowed a bee.'

At night, we buried our water-bottles in the sand and, by morning, the water would be almost ice cold. As he crawled back to his vehicle Don said, 'I'll fix your back, Kev.'

'How?'

'Like this,' and he chucked a mug of water over him. Kev's back straightened up stiff as a board. He let fly a fusillade of swearing as the whole troop collapsed into fits of laughter.

This wasn't the last time that Kev faced a problem with medication. A few years later, stricken with constipation, he'd gone to the MO for help. The doctor gave him some enormous suppositories to ease things along. A couple of days later, Kev returned.

'How are the guts, Kevin?'

'Still the same. For all the good them pills have done, I might as well have shoved 'em up me arse!'

That evening, as night fell again in the open desert, the perennial problem of officers evacuating their bowels in the presence of the common soldiery reared its ugly head, so to speak. Willy Fyfe, our twenty-year-old troop commander, took himself quietly off into the privacy of the desert for his evening constitutional and was straining hard when evil Corporal Springles nailed him with one of the vehicle search-lights.

We set off early next morning and, around ten o'clock, stopped for a brew. *Whooooooosh!* A pair of Hawker Hunters appeared from nowhere and screamed over us before pulling up into a steep climb. The pilot came up on the radio. 'Gotcha that time, Don!'

They certainly had. As they circled he called us again: 'Line up your vehicles and I'll take a photo.'

We lined them up and he came over again, so low that the picture shows me covering my ears against the noise.

Taff Springles, still pleased with himself for catching Willy with his pants down, now ostentatiously went for a dump. He casually dropped his kecks and squatted down, giving it full steam ahead, but then leaped to his feet.

'AAAARGH! FUCKING HELL!'

Alas, poor Taff: being notably well hung, his enormous cobblers had made contact with a sizzling rock, raising a blister half as large again.

After three weeks or so, the fun and games came to an end and we drove to El Adem to prepare for our return to the UK. Checking on a map I saw that we were only twenty miles or so from Tobruk, so I borrowed one of the Pinkies and a few of us headed on down to the military cemetery there, a relic of the Second World War.

I'm not sure why, maybe just sentimentality or superstition, but wherever we were in the world, we always made an effort to visit any British military cemeteries nearby. And there always seemed to be one.

Lucky D Squadron, we were back in Hereford for Christmas and the New Year, but soon afterwards we started receiving briefings and updates on the situation in Aden in the expectation that we would soon be out there. Of course, normal training had to continue at the same time, and as the troop medic I was put on the annual update and refresher course run out of Training Wing. This period of individual training was always a chance to unwind, not because the training was easy, but because you got most evenings and weekends free. This gave a chance for 'normality' to reassert itself in our lives, although actually, of course, our normality usually meant flogging around some jungle or desert: the domestic routine of life in Hereford was something we only occasionally got to experience.

So it came to pass one evening that Kevin and I had adjourned to the Imperial after work and were just getting around the outside of our second pint on a chilly February evening when Lofty Wiseman – a corporal in A Squadron – came in. He was still in uniform and grinning all over his face as he walked over to us.

'All right lads? There's free beer for D Squadron back at the camp. Want a lift?' He made off towards another group of D Squadron lads leaving us to consider his invitation.

'For fuck's sake . . .' Kev's reaction was no big surprise, but it was an offer we couldn't refuse. We both took a last big gulp of bitter and headed outside where Lofty had left the duty short-wheelbase Land Rover with the engine ticking over. I climbed in the front seat and Kevin – the airborne wart – clambered over the tailgate into the back, still chuntering and swearing.

Lofty jumped back into the driving seat, crunched the Rover into first gear, floored the accelerator and we took off into Hereford, cornering on two wheels as we hurtled through the narrow streets, stopping off at pubs, restaurants and houses, giving D Squadron the good news. In the front I was able to grab hold of the dashboard as Lofty threw the vehicle around, but in the back, Kev was being bounced around like a rubber ball. 'Fuckin' 'ell, Loft, at this rate you'll kill us before we fuckin' get there!'

By the time we reached camp, the party was in full swing in D Squadron basha which had become a hive of purposeful activity. As I headed for the locker room, one of the lads told me: 'On the square, ready to be on the buses at 2000 hours, Pete.' Looking at my watch I saw that we had just over an hour to be ready. No problem. Like everyone else in the squadron, I kept a complete duplicate set of operational kit ready to go in my locker. All I had to do was get my civvies off and squared away, pack a few extra bits and pieces into a holdall and I was ready to go.

Free beer: not a piss-up this time but the codeword for a rapid deployment by the designated 'quick-move' squadron of 22 SAS. Operation Flashbulb.

So at 2000, there we all were, ready to pile into the three old army charabancs which had drawn up on the parade ground in Bradbury Lines. Dressed in our lightweight jungle green uniforms, we had our windproofs and para smocks thrown on over the top to keep us warm on the trip down to the RAF airfield at Lyneham in Wiltshire. By now, the three-tonners with the squadron kit were already on their way, taking weapons, ammunition, radios and rations out to the airfield for onward transport to our final destination.

One of the things about the SAS is that the soldiers are generally older than you find in the rest of the army. In my troop, 18 Troop, the average age at this time was around thirty-two and this means more of the lads are married and settled down. So although there was a buzz of adrenaline in the air, there was also the sadness of separation from wives and young children. For most of the trip to Lyneham many of the lads were sitting quietly, smoking and thinking about home.

At Lyneham, we piled aboard an RAF Britannia and within two hours of the codeword being passed we were airborne, racing from the icy cold of February in the Welsh border country towards the southernmost tip of Arabia.

Engine trouble in the Britannia aircraft meant it took us three days to reach Aden, but gave us time to sort ourselves out into our nondescript operational uniforms, and when we arrived at the airport we expected to be able to deploy quickly up country, without the locals realizing who we were. Our briefing had been that the deployment was covert, 'Top Secret' even, but things didn't quite work out as planned. Somewhat to our surprise, Joe Schofield, the quartermaster, turned up to greet us at RAF Khormaksar dressed in his SAS 'pea greens', complete with SAS beret, wings, stable belt and shoulder titles. As this was sinking in, an announcement came over the airport tannoy, welcoming the 'new arrivals from the SAS Regiment'.

I happened to be standing next to Lofty Large, and heard him chuntering away: 'Fucking thanks for that, Joe, you prat...' To be honest, it's often unrealistic to keep a deployment of that sort completely secret, but even so, we did feel that they might have made a bit of an effort . . .

The next day we flew up country in an RAF Beverley to Al Milah, a small village on the road from Aden to Dalah. This was a camp for the Royal Engineers unit that maintained the road, a graded track rather than a motorway. It was based a few hundred metres from the village, which consisted of mud and rock-built buildings and a small fort occupied by the local police force. The camp itself was literally just that: tents, a vehicle and plant park for the Sappers' equipment and a helicopter pad, all surrounded by a barbed-wire entanglement to keep out any unwanted visitors. Our job was to mount a series of day observation posts and night ambushes in the hope of pinning down and then, with luck, finishing off a gaggle of Arab terrorists who were operating in the area: sniping at soldiers and police, rocketing and mortaring military bases, and laying mines on the roads.

Of course, this was not the first time that D Squadron had been to Aden, but since then we'd been on jungle operations in Borneo, followed by winter in Hereford, and we all looked as white as sheets, whilst the Sappers who shared our camp were tanned a deep brown from working outside during the day wearing just their shorts and boots. As we lined up for our first meal in the cookhouse after we arrived, one of the Catering Corps cooks remarked to Don Large: 'Just got here, mate? Wait until you get up the sharp end.' Don looked down at his own pale skin and replied, 'Son, you ought to see it from the inside.' The cook got the message.

We settled in for the night in our accommodation, which turned out to be marquee tents with a ditch at the end for us all to get into in the event of any unpleasantness. This wasn't long in coming. We'd been in bed a few hours when we heard the metallic cough of mortars being launched. No big surprise, we were all awake instantaneously. Kevin, our resident mortar expert, gave us the verdict from his scratcher.

'Don't worry, lads, I'm an instructor. They're not coming this way.'

His pronouncement was followed by the eerie whistle of the bombs coming down.

'Fuckin' 'ell!'

There was a scrambling sound as we dived for the trench. In the middle of the pitch black tent I crashed into the airborne wart.

'Thanks for your advice there, Kevin.'

'Don't fuckin' mention it.'

Not too far away, the first bombs exploded, and we heard the patter of dirt and spent shrapnel hitting the canvas.

It was a feature of operations in the Aden Protectorate, as it has been in other terrorist campaigns involving the British Army like Northern Ireland, that the enemy, in themselves, don't present much of a problem. Once we were in contact with them, their training, tactics and equipment were so poor that we would almost always come off better than they would, except on occasions where British troops were greatly outnumbered. Militarily poor as they were, they weren't stupid. And, as a result, the biggest problem we faced was finding them. Over the two or three years of trouble that had preceded our deployment, the terrorists had developed a fairly good knowledge of British Army techniques – good enough, anyway, to recognize when trouble was brewing – and as soon as they sensed that anything was up, they got out of the way sharpish. That's terrorists for you, though: it isn't in their interests or capabilities to take on regular troops if they can avoid them, and as far as they're concerned, why should they?

So the key to successful operations was surprise. If we could get in amongst them before they'd cottoned on to the fact that we were there, then we could sort them out, but it required forethought and subtlety.

One of the benefits of the SAS's multi-skilled approach to squadron organization is that there is a wide variety of ways in which the soldiers can be inserted into the operational area. Mountain Troop can lead the squadron up sheer slopes; Air Troop can insert by freefall parachute to mark a DZ for subsequent parachute or helicopter insertion; Boat Troop can bring us in in their Zodiac or Gemini assault craft. Alternatively, as we did for this operation, we can all get in the backs of the RCT's Stalwart trucks as they're moving off in a convoy, then leap out when they're close enough to the area we're trying to get to.

On the day after we arrived we found ourselves quietly climbing into the backs of the Stalwarts in the late afternoon, ready to deploy for an eight-day operation into the hills once darkness fell. What we knew about the enemy was this: there were two gangs of between twenty and thirty terrorists operating between us at Al Milah, Habilayn further to the north, and the Darla road. They were armed with small-arms and light support weapons, like mortars and rocket launchers, and their task was to keep the security forces' heads down whilst they covered the movement of weapons and explosives into Aden city. Our job was to stop them.

We sat quietly waiting in the backs of the Stalwarts until after last light when the convoy formed up and we moved off. Our area of operations had been picked from the map: we were to be dropped at a bend in the road where the convoy would have to slow down anyway, but which opened onto the mouth of a wadi up which the squadron would move before making for an RV, splitting up and occupying daytime OP positions, which had also been selected from the map.

There's a saying in the army, 'Time spent on reconnaissance is seldom wasted,' and that's true, particularly in special forces operations, but by the same token, careless recce can give away your intentions to a vigilant enemy. It was safe to select the RV and OP sites from the map because the headshed trusted us to change them if we arrived there and found they weren't suitable.

From the Stalwarts, we made our way into cover as best we could, staggering under the weight of upwards of a hundred pounds of kit. The idea was that we were going to be on the ground for six to eight days, in half-troop (eight men) strength, and clearly this meant carrying a good deal of gear. The terrorists' standard operating procedure was that their lead scout would carry a hand-held rocket launcher to give them firepower if they got bumped, and to counteract this, our leading scout, in this case me, carried a light machine-gun (the old .303 Bren gun, converted to Nato 7.62 calibre). The weapon itself was nineteen and a half pounds, and with it went ten fully loaded magazines, carried in a vest, but there was the rest of my kit as well: two one-gallon plastic water containers at ten pounds weight each; my two water bottles; six to ten days' rations; a selection of grenades (fragmentation, smoke and white phosphorus); batteries for the A41 radio; and finally, of course, the troop medical pack. We also had to carry Paddy's kit; weighed down by the bulky radio he had little room for his own gear.

We began the approach march to the squadron RV in a long column, led by 16 Troop, D Squadron's free-fallers. The troop commander was Robin Letts who, apart from being blind as a bat, had never operated in these desert/mountain conditions before. His previous operational experience was entirely in Borneo and, as a consequence, he set off extremely slowly, moving at jungle pace and checking his navigation all the time, all of which was entirely unnecessary. With the huge loads we were carrying, we didn't want to wait around. Eventually the 16 Troop sergeant, Mick Reeves, got on to him on the short-range walkie-talkie.

'Come on, sir, you've got to get your arse in gear. We're not in the bleedin' jungle now.'

'Oh, I'm frightfully sorry, Sergeant Reeves!'

Mick took over as 'column leader' and the pace began to pick up, but something was bothering Robin, now at the back of 16 Troop. A reedy whisper came over the walkie-talkie on Mick's chest.

'Sergeant Reeves, Sergeant Reeves.'

Mick was busy concentrating on the route ahead and ignored him.

'Sergeant Reeves, Sergeant Reeves!' It was a little more insistent this time, but Mick continued to ignore it as he tried to sort out some problem with the troop, though he began to mutter something about 'stupid fucking officers'.

'Sergeant Reeves, Sergeant Reeves!' Robin's voice was now coming dangerously loudly through everyone's walkie-talkies.

Mick finally lost his rag: 'WHAT?'

As Mick's bellow echoed amongst the boulders, the entire squadron took cover, with everyone thinking, What the hell was that, then?

With order restored, we reached the RV and broke down into our half-troops, making off at speed for our prearranged OP positions on the mountain tops. It was crucial that we got there before first light so that our positions weren't compromised and we did need time to build protective sangars.* At the same time, a blind rush might have got us killed. In the jungle, visibility is such that members of a patrol are rarely more than five or ten metres apart – any more and they lose sight of each other – but in these conditions, the lead scout needed to be right out in front so that if he came across an ambush, the rest of the patrol had a chance of surviving it, and hopefully of rescuing the scout as well!

The problem was that the ground lent itself very well to ambushes. The only places where it was relatively easy to move were in the beds of wadis, but the sides of the wadis consisted of a range of broken boulders, cliff-faces, scree slopes, ledges, fissures and even smaller wadis, any of which could conceal an ambush party. Fortunately, a successful ambush requires some preparation, and throughout our first tour we got away with it.

By pushing ourselves we reached our position with time to spare and began the hard slog of building sangars from the loose rocks and boulders that were lying around. The purpose of the sangars wasn't just to conceal us but also to give us a measure of protection against small arms fire and mortar fragments. On TV and films, you see this and that weapon being described as 'high velocity' or 'high-powered', and you see the heroes in gun battles dodging behind dustbins and car doors when they come under fire. The truth is that real high-velocity rounds – the sort you fire from rifles and machine-guns – will go through an obstacle such as a

---

* A defensive position constructed above ground.

car door like a hot knife through butter. With a GPMG or a Bren gun and a couple of hundred rounds of ammunition – not very much really – you could demolish a decent-sized semi-detached house in a couple of minutes. Consequently, our sangars weren't going to be much use to us with walls less than about a metre thick and it took some effort to get them built when we arrived at our site.

But thanks to Lofty's inspired leadership, we did make it to our designated OP site in good time, and this despite the presence of our troop commander, Willy Fyfe, who'd arrived during our build-up training.

One of the things you find in the SAS is that a significant minority of the lads have little time for officers, or the junior ones anyway. The reasons for this vary, but it's basically down to the fact that a young guy with a couple of years' experience of regular operations comes into the troop, supposedly as its 'commander', over people who have been there much longer and who have a vastly greater range of skills. The army's the army, and you do what you're told, provided it isn't completely barking, but some of the officers who've come into the Regiment were definitely not up to the job. But, having said that, officers who didn't have much experience of hard soldiering had other attributes that made up for it: a university education, for example. Willy Fyfe was all of twenty years old when he joined the squadron and was placed in command of a troop that included men who'd been in combat in Malaya when he was still in short trousers, but he was fit, intelligent and keen to learn – and, by and large, he was prepared to listen to the advice of people like Lofty and not interfere too much.

But all we learned on that first job was how hot it could get. During the day we sat there, two men to a sangar, hidden under a camouflage net made from six 'face veils' sewn together, observing the low ground, valleys and wadi beds through our binos and being gently roasted as the temperature climbed to around 130° Fahrenheit. We were looking for any movement: men, mules and camel trains. At night we cached our heavy equipment in the sangars and scrambled down into the valleys and wadis to place ambushes on likely enemy routes. Again, even with just our belt order, this was no easy task, because the ground was so broken and boulder-strewn. But that first time out, none of the enemy showed up and we returned to Al Milah empty-handed.

In between operations the form was much the same as in Borneo. A couple of days to rest and recuperate before beginning the battle procedure for the next op. The big difference lay in how we spent our relaxation time. In Borneo we were based in Kuching, a relatively large and safe town with bars and restaurants where we could get into our civvies, go out for a meal and some beers, and wind down away from the military environment. In Aden, when we were up country at any rate, we were effectively confined to tented military camps whenever we weren't on operations, which was a little more constricting. Still, we made the best of it, drinking and eating together in makeshift messes and, in the evenings, watching film shows projected onto a big screen outside the cookhouse tent.

The film shows were popular, not only with us but with the locals as well: they would congregate outside the wire to watch the proceedings from a distance. The big favourites for them were Westerns, during which they would inevitably be cheering for the Indians, but woe betide us if the action was too one-sided. During one scene of slaughter, as the US cavalry dealt with a particularly fierce Indian band, one of the lads went round the back of the screen for a piss and noticed that small holes were appearing in the fabric. He ran back to order the projectionist to switch it off and, sure enough, in the absence of the film soundtrack we could hear the crack and thump of terrorist sniper fire ranging in on us. So that was the end of the show for that night.

But the terrorists were much more than a mere irritant. At 0600 the next morning we were lying on our camp-beds when we heard some small-arms fire off in the distance. It wasn't until our briefing two hours later that we discovered what had happened. Two of the young Sappers from the camp had gone down to the village to fill the water bowser from the well that the Engineers had dug. It was something they did every morning and, from the purist's point of view, it was a mistake because they were setting a pattern the terrorist could learn from. On this particular morning, the terrorists had set a simple ambush, and as the soldiers went about their work, they were machine-gunned at close range. One died, the other was severely wounded. As they lay there, the terrorists had calmly taken their weapons and made off. It was a repulsive murder – not least because the Sappers had dug the well for the benefit of the villagers – but in one respect it helped us: we now knew that there was a terrorist group in our area.

For the next operation we were fairly quick off the mark, insofar as we were following up on the two murders. The format of the op was much the same: we deployed out at night and occupied hilltop OPs in half-troop strength, then waited to see what we could see. This time it wasn't long in coming. Some time in the late afternoon we heard a loud outbreak of firing from one of the other half-troop locations and Paddy, listening in on the set, told us: '16 Troop's got a contact!'

What had happened was that one of the OPs had spotted a group of enemy on the move and half of 16 Troop, the free-fall boys, had been scooped up in a helicopter to intercept them. Unfortunately, as the result of some kind of cock-up, they'd been put in too close and Swede Smith, a sergeant in the troop, had collected an explosive round through his shoulder.

As it happened, the rest of Swede's half-troop were all ex-Parachute Regiment soldiers, infantrymen well drilled in the basics of ground warfare, and with Swede down, they executed a perfect section attack, killing two of the terrorists and taking the position from them.

Whilst this was going on, Lofty was calmly getting the troop ready for the inevitable lift out to go and help 16 Troop. This was what you got with Lofty: he didn't wait for orders, he anticipated them, so when the chopper appeared a few minutes later, we were already down at the LZ with kit packed, weapons ready and everything in order.

Thirty seconds or so later, we'd been dropped off on a ridge-line much closer to the action, and now we were really in amongst it as the scattered terrorists attempted to use their firepower to dig themselves out of trouble. This was little Willy Fyfe's first action and he was a bit overawed by what was happening, but Lofty quickly asserted control, offering to take his half of the troop forward to engage the enemy. Leaving Willy to the rear in support we moved off – Lofty, me, Big Ron Adey, Johnny Partridge and Hughie, our token American (a Good Ole Boy from the deep South on attachment from the Green Berets, who'd come on operations with us against the strict orders of the Pentagon).

We trotted towards the little peak closest to where the fighting was taking place and Lofty went forward to check it was clear. When he'd done that, he signalled to the rest of us to come on forward, with me, carrying the Bren, giving cover from the rear. As Ron and I got closer, we were suddenly enveloped in a hail of dust, rock splinters and noise as a long burst of machine-gun fire hit around us.

'JESUS CHRIST!' We started running like the clappers and got down amongst the rocks where Lofty was waiting, looking slightly apologetic.

'Sorry about that, lads, I could've sworn there was none of 'em down there. Still,' he consoled himself, 'you can't be right all the time.'

Ron started laughing, much to Lofty's puzzlement.

'What's the matter? Why's he laughing?'

'Because he's still alive, Lofty.'

There was still a lot of shooting going on but, frustratingly, we couldn't see precisely where the enemy were so Lofty wanted the rest of the troop to come up and reinforce our position. Unfortunately, Willy decided to put his foot down. Punchy, the squadron commander, was busy bringing up more support for 16 Troop and didn't have time to micromanage our troop commander who, rather helpfully, came up on the net saying, 'I'm twenty-one today, and someone's shooting at me for the first time in my life!'

Despite this interesting information, he wouldn't let Lofty bring the rest of the troop up to where we were, simply because Punchy hadn't told him to. Lofty's idea was for us to get closer in to the firefight and then, maybe, put in an attack on the enemy's flank, but with just the five of us, it was a non-starter.

Poor old Willy. He wasn't Lofty's favourite officer that day and it was a while before Lofty could bring himself to refer to him without using an adjective beginning with the letter 'F'.

So, with our flanking assault ruled out, Lofty now decided to try to find some targets for us to engage. The machine-gun that had fired on me and Ron had been quite close, but it hadn't fired again and our assumption was that it had been somebody trying to do what we'd done – get to the high ground – and that he'd buggered off when he saw we'd beaten him to it. Then we saw a little group of them about 500 metres away, part of the gang who were shooting it out with 16 Troop. Lofty gave me a target indication and I put in a few bursts but they were too far away to be good targets and I don't think I hit more than two of them at the most.

It's an interesting thing, but one of the questions you get asked by people who haven't been soldiers is, 'Have you ever killed anybody?' That may seem straightforward, but the truth is that very few soldiers can put their hands on their hearts and say, 'Yes, I have killed x number of people.' The reason for this is simple: most of the time you're too far away to know. Certainly I've shot at people who have then gone down, but you can rarely tell if that's because they've been killed, wounded, fallen over in shock or simply dived for cover. Even on the Koemba ambush in Borneo, at a range of less than fifty metres, I couldn't say for sure if I hit anybody. I probably did – that's all I can say – and they probably died.

But whether I hit them or not, a couple of bursts was enough to get the terrorists moving into cover sharpish and we now needed another means of getting at them. This wasn't long in coming. One of the Wessex helicopters had brought in a mortar crew and Lofty began to bring fire down on the enemy. Once the mortar crew had got the range, Lofty gave the targets a real stonking, and when the smoke and dust cleared we were surprised to see one of the terrorists staggering about dizzily in the impact area, apparently unhurt. He made a fairly straightforward target and I offered to knock him over with the Bren, but Lofty, who'd been on the wrong end of similar bombardments in Korea, was obviously feeling charitable.

'If he can survive that he deserves a break. Let him go.'

Around now, the chopper carrying Swede went past close enough for us to see splashes of blood on the windows but the firefight didn't seem to be going terribly well, mainly because of the problem we were having locating the enemy. Lofty decided that desperate measures called for desperate solutions: he decided to offer himself as a target in the hope of getting one of the enemy snipers to reveal his position. He pulled the camouflage cover off his walkie-talkie antenna, stood up on a rock and waved it in the sunlight, while we watched and listened. There was a loud *crack!* and an explosive bullet hit the ground a few inches from Lofty's feet, and not all that far from Hughie the Yank's head.

'Jesus, Lofty, do you have to do that?' was Hughie's reaction.

'Don't worry, they're lousy shots, they'll never get me.'

'Yeah, but what if they miss you and get me?' came the pained response. Lofty thought about this for a few seconds then hopped down from the rock, back into cover. Hughie looked over at me and said, 'Scholey, I've never come across so many complete fucking lunatics in one place at the same time.'

Well, with one thing and another, it had been a tough day.

By now we had word from the radio that a pair of RAF Hunter fighter-bombers were on their way to give us a bit of close air support. Lofty got back on the net to call them in while the rest of us watched from cover. In the crystal-clear mountain air we could see them coming from miles away, silhouetted against the azure sky. Watching, Johnny Partridge remarked, 'Don't they look amazing . . . Jesus! They're coming straight for us!'

I managed to fumble out my air-marker panel and hold it up to show them where we were and Lofty gave them a target indication. After a bit of chit-chat, they came screeching in to strafe the terrorists, and the last thing the pilot said was, 'You'd better keep your heads down, my shell cases will give you a nasty bump.'

The two planes roared in at us and opened fire with their 30mm cannons a little way short of where we were, before screeching overhead and pulling up. The sound of aircraft was suddenly replaced by the noise of the empty brass shell-cases clanging on the rocks around us. They were heavy enough to kill you if they landed on you so we found what cover we could. After several more passes at the enemy position, the Hunters roared off back towards Khormaksar.

By now the quick reaction force of Royal Marines had deployed from Habilayn, and the SAS half-troops were ordered to pull back onto the ridge lines to act as a picket, ready to hit any terrorists who were flushed out by the boot-necks. One of the 16 Troop picket teams saw movement way off in the distance.

Les was first off the mark. 'Look, lads, it's a terrorist.'

We strained to see what he was pointing at and, sure enough, about 600 yards away we could make out a small khaki-clad figure. Brian Dodd had got hold of one of the new Armalite AR15 rifles before the op – a 5.56mm lightweight weapon with the capability of firing fully automatic, but not really suitable for long-range work – and he now eased it into the aim, even though his target was about 300 metres beyond what was thought to be the normal effective range.

'You'll never get him.'

'No problem, mate!'

Bri gently squeezed off a shot and, sure enough, the terrorist went down.

'Great shot, mate, well done!'

We were pretty chuffed with Brian, but it wasn't long before word came back that the 'terrorist' was actually a

Marine who'd strayed into our area, and had collected a flesh wound in his thigh for his trouble. Oh, shit.

As dusk began to fall, the squadron got the order to pull out. By now we'd cleared through the location and retrieved the bodies of the dead terrorists, as well as scraps of information from documents they'd been carrying and a selection of weapons, including the rifles taken from the two Sappers. One problem that had arisen in Aden was that the terrorists had occasionally mutilated the bodies of their own dead then claimed that we'd done it as propaganda. This meant that if we did get a kill, we had to get the bodies back to HQ and out of the way a.s.a.p. As we were shaking out for our return to camp, a Scout helicopter flew in to collect the dead, and Punchy told Derek Gorman to escort them back.

Unfortunately, once the bodies were piled on the helicopter it became clear that there was no room for the escort, much to Derek's relief.

'Ah, sorry, boss, looks like the pilot'll just have to run 'em back on his own, then.'

'I don't think so, Derek. They're not going to mind if you sit on top of them.'

'Fucking hell, you don't just have to chase them halfway round Arabia, you've got to turn the bastards into furniture as well!'

Well, it was a result but certainly only a partial one, and this became a kind of pattern for operations in the next three months. When we did get to grips with the enemy, we overwhelmed them, but they had very little interest in taking us on on an even basis. As far as they were concerned, the slightest success – a dead or wounded British soldier, or an attack carried out without serious loss – was a major propaganda coup. Whenever we made contact, the terrorists' first inclination was to get the hell out of it as quickly as possible.

We flew out to Habilayn and went to the Naafi for a few beers to wind down. While we were sitting there, replaying the events of the day, members of the Marines' Quick Reaction Force came in and, naturally, we called them over to join us. Brian Dodd was mortified that he'd shot the Marine, even though it wasn't his fault in any real sense, but when we raised the subject with the young booties, they weren't too bothered.

'Actually, mate, you done us a favour.'

'Why was that?'

'The bloke you shot is the drill sergeant.'

This certainly explained their blasé attitude. The Marine thought for a few moments and then added, '. . . and actually, it was a pretty good shot, at that range.'

Brian wasn't having this. 'No, mate, it was crap.'

'Why?'

'I was aiming for his other leg.'

Brian was actually a tremendous soldier and he earned the Military Medal for his actions that day, but he didn't always manage to maintain his sense of humour. Back in Hereford he'd bought himself an old Austin Seven, which he completely renovated over a period of about eight months, spending all his spare time and money on it. Having finished the bloody thing, he was enormously proud of it and made sure everyone in the squadron knew what he'd achieved.

One afternoon, around the time when he was finally finishing his great project, Jock Thompson and I were walking down to Hereford for a pint when we heard a sound like a foghorn going off behind us. We looked around and saw Brian, pleased as punch, sitting in his car and letting off the klaxon.

'Want a lift, lads?'

'That's very kind of you, mate.'

We piled in and he set off, extolling the virtues of his pet car. As we reached the Wye Bridge he said, 'Okay, lads, where shall I drop you? The city centre?'

'No thanks, Bri, the back of Woolies will do.'

'Why there?' asked Brian.

'It's secluded and we don't want to be seen getting out of this fucking jalopy.'

With this Brian slammed on the brakes. 'You bastards, get out and fucking walk!'

Like many officers, Willie Fyfe didn't stay with the troop very long, not because he wasn't up to it but because the Regiment moved him on to other tasks. Later in that Aden tour, though, his time with the troop was cut short in a highly dramatic way. We were acting as the 'Crash Rescue Team' on standby when a signal came in from an infantry call sign in an area called Cap Badge Ridge. The message was that a group of the enemy had been seen going into a large cave.

Two choppers were ready, 18 Troop – us – with light weapons were to fly into the area, drop off and investigate and, in the meantime 19 Troop – the Mountain Troop – were to go on to Cap Badge Ridge itself and ready themselves to give us support using machine-guns and a 'Carl Gustav' anti-tank weapon.

We had a good look around, but couldn't find the cave at first. Eventually, some distance below us, we saw what might be a cave entrance. Willy decided to go down and investigate.

'Scholey,' he called, because, like a prat, I was standing closest to him, 'you and I will climb down and if it is a cave we'll go in and shout to them to surrender. If they don't obey, I'll throw in an M26 hand grenade.'

This struck me as a very bad idea, but that wasn't all: he then told me to get my bright orange air marker panel and drape it around my neck. I could see the rest of the troop laughing and taking the piss out of me, but I wasn't going to take this lying down.

'Why do you want me to do that, Willy?'

'So that 19 Troop can see from their position that we're not the enemy and won't fire on us down there,' he replied.

'But any enemy in the area will spot me a mile away. I'll have more shit fired at me than they did at Dunkirk, so if you don't mind, piss off!' I said.

'That's an order.'

'I don't give a shit. It might be an order, but it's not a lawful command.'

'You're a coward,' he said.

I said just two words to him: 'YOU'RE CORRECT!'

By this time the troop were having fits of laughter behind his back. He then said, 'Okay, no panel.'

Now I had a suggestion.

'Instead of a hand grenade let's get the anti-tank weapon over from 19 Troop. Put that into the cave and it'll certainly get their back teeth rattling.'

'No,' said Willy, fiercely. 'It's my job to go in.'

With that, he pulled out the grenade and half withdrew the pin, ready for rapid use.

Unfortunately, it had been raining very heavily for a few days and the rocks were still very wet. We were wearing Clark's desert boots, which were fine when the ground was dry, but highly dangerous in slippery conditions. There was a ledge in the rock which we had to manoeuvre across before we could descend to the so-called cave. Willy said, 'I'll go first, you follow.'

As he began to scramble across I could see how slippery it was. I started to say to him, 'You're going to fall.'

He'd just said, 'No, I'm not,' when he fell, sliding about three hundred metres down a sloping scree field towards the lip of a cliff. He managed to grab hold of a small bush, which saved him from going over.

One of the lads shouted, 'The bastard's dead!'

A thin, indignant voice from below shouted up, 'No, I'm not!'

Taff Springles called over, 'Come on, Pete, we'd better get down there and get him.'

'Hang on five seconds,' shouted Kev. 'He's got a grenade with the pin half out and it has a five-second fuse.'

As this was going on 19 Troop Command came up on the radio.

'We've seen movement through the binos. What's happening?'

'Our Sunray's just fallen off the cliff,' Taff answered.

'Is he okay?'

'We don't know, he ain't reached the bottom yet,' said Taff.

Eventually Taff and I got him and, with some difficulty, brought him back up. As well as the cuts and bruises you'd expect, he clearly had a broken collar-bone. As we watched the helicopter take him to hospital Kev broke the silence.

'Now,' he said, 'the troop can get back to normal.'

In between operations, we occasionally got to go down to Aden town for some R and R, which gave us plenty of opportunities for serious misbehaviour. One time, after we'd cleaned and stowed our kit, Kev and I decided to take ourselves off on a crawl round the officers' and sergeants' mess bars of all the garrison units. We were chancing it a bit because we were both still troopers in the SAS, but we reckoned what the hell, and went for it, and we found that we were welcomed in some, got slung out of others and generally had a good old time. The last place we went to was the sergeants' mess of the Royal Anglians where, it turned out, they were having a smart function for members and their wives, with everyone dolled up in tropical mess kit and evening dresses. Unfortunately, Kev and I were just wearing shorts, and as we made our way to the bar, the duty sergeant ran up to us.

'Oy, you two! Where are you from?'

We told him the name of our camp and he realized we were SAS. 'Well, you can't come in here with those shorts on!' he continued. I think as he said it he realized he was making a mistake, because as all attention switched to us, Kev and I had the same idea.

'Fair enough,' Kev replied, and we both whipped our shorts down – we weren't wearing underpants – and did a runner. This got us hauled in front of Punchy the next day and we were both fined ten shillings, though he did tell us that the wives were hoping we'd go back the next day for an encore.

Aden was also the first time that the Regiment had really dipped its toes into urban counter-terrorist operations. The commanding officer at that time was John Slim – son of the Second World War Field Marshal Sir William Slim and a soldier with real vision. He had seen the potential for small and flexible special forces units and had encouraged members of the Regiment to acquire a range of special skills which could be passed on within the SAS, thus expanding the number of tasks we could fulfil and guaranteeing our continued usefulness in an ever-changing world.

One of these skills was close quarter battle with the 9mm Browning pistol, which was standard issue for staff officers, military policemen and so forth, but had never really been considered as anything other than a joke in the rest of the army because of its supposed short range and inaccuracy. In fact, encouraged by John Slim and led by Alec Spence, the Regiment had adopted a system which turned the Browning into a real aggressive weapon, combining a rapid draw technique, instinctive aiming and the 'double-tap' (squeezing the trigger twice) as well as various kicks and punches to keep the opposition clear of the weapon itself. This formed the basis of SAS armed undercover and bodyguard skills, which have subsequently been used in Northern Ireland and elsewhere. In Aden, it gave members of the Regiment the ability, when suitably disguised as Arabs, to lurk around the streets and alleyways of the city in the hope of nailing the urban bomb-throwers and assassins who were prosecuting the campaign there. Although I was never personally involved in this side of our operations in Aden, by all accounts they were notably effective, even though one of the more dangerous threats the lads faced was from undercover squads of the various infantry battalions who were attempting to do the same thing over the same ground.

While we waited for our flights home, we were living in flats, four to a room, in downtown Aden. We spent our spare time shopping locally and doing a bit of socializing, winding down after the tensions of the tour with friends we had made while we were out there.

I was sharing a room with Kev, Taff Brown and Paddy Millikin. Poor old Taff had terrible piles and was waiting to have an operation when we got home, but in the meantime was using some ointment to keep the pain at bay. He administered it by inserting the tube into his arse and giving it a good squirt. We also shared lockers, two to each locker. I shared with Paddy, Kev with Taff.

Taff had just finished with the tube of cream when the lights failed. Meanwhile, Kev was having a shower ready to go out to dinner with some friends. He had his shower and shave, but forgot his toothpaste. Rushing back into the darkened room, he put his hand into his locker and got his toothpaste, as he thought.

He came back in spitting and spluttering. Before he could say anything, Taff said, 'Kev, why have you pinched my pile cream?'

Kev said, 'Pinched it? I've eaten half the fucking tube!'

He used half a bottle of whisky to wash his mouth out.

Our first operational tour in Aden culminated, as usual, in a somewhat raucous party which was held, for some reason, in the Irish Guards' Naafi two days before we were due to fly home. It was some time after midnight when in walked the Guards' battalion orderly sergeant: a huge creaking mass of bullshit in his highly polished boots, tropical number two dress with razor creases on trousers that came to just above his ankles, a red sash, a cheese-cutter cap with a peak so slashed it was resting on the bridge of his nose, and, of all things, a swagger stick. He came over to where we were happily partying and, instead of accepting the various jovial offers of drinks, and not realizing that our squadron commander was there, poked Jock Thompson in the back with his swagger stick and screamed, in true Guards NCO style, 'What are you lot doing in 'ere? The Naafi should have closed an hour ago!'

As he drew himself up to his full height and prepared his second volley, Jock snatched the swagger stick from under his arm and snapped it over his knee. The Guardsman stood there, his mouth hanging open like a goldfish on Mogadon, as someone else whipped his cap off and poured a pint of beer into it – at which point it was suggested that he might like to fuck off. He ran from the Naafi and we carried on partying.

Unfortunately, ten minutes later he was back, this time

with some members of the barrack guard in tow, screaming and raving as they stood laughing at him behind his back. Our RSM got up and ushered us out and we went quietly as the bullshit king continued his rant. It didn't end there, however. The Irish Guards' hierarchy worked themselves up into a stew about the whole situation and demanded court-martials and sackings, but our headshed quietly told them to get stuffed and nothing came of it.

Our second operational tour of Aden, which began in April 1967, was, if anything, even more frustrating than the first. When we'd deployed on Operation Flashbulb, the political situation was confused but comprehensible: Aden and the Protectorate would become independent, but Britain would retain her bases there and continue to use it as the Headquarters Middle East. In effect, this meant that Britain guaranteed the defence of Aden against any outside aggressor and gave local politicians a stake in maintaining British friendship, trust and support, and in assisting the British against the Yemeni-sponsored guerrillas of the National Liberation Front and the People's Front for the Liberation of South Yemen. But in the spring of 1966, Harold Wilson's Labour government announced that, for financial reasons, Britain would be leaving Aden completely after independence. As the implications of this sank in, it became every man for himself and the security situation began to spiral out of control. The reasons for this were straightforward: if the British weren't going to be there after independence, nobody had any stake in supporting us, so why bother?

The pattern of up-country operations was much the same as before. Deploying to high ground to maintain observation on the valley floors and wadis then moving in to ambush by night. One operation, out of Habilayn, involved us in cordoning off a village near the border which was suspected of harbouring terrorists. I was paired with Taff Brown, often known as Bent-legs because of his bandy legs. As we approached the village, there was a sudden burst of fire from in front of us and we hit the deck as rounds started pinging from the rocks all around us. I was carrying a GPMG, and as we ducked for cover I shouted to Taff, 'Quick, you get down there. I'll get behind this rock with the gympy.'

I settled down behind a big, comfortable, solid, bullet-proof rock as Taff gingerly made his way forward towards slightly more dubious cover. There was another burst all round us and Taff looked back to ask, 'Scholey, are you going to return their fire or what?'

'Why would I want to do that? It'll only annoy them.'

'Scholey, you are lower than a rattlesnake's belly!'

On the same operation we had another funny experience when we stopped a minibus near the village. The occupants were being a bit stroppy and one of our guys fired a warning burst close enough to their heads to gain their instant attention, at which point one of the Arabs started complaining in a strong Brummie accent. He turned out to be a worker from the car factory at Longbridge who'd come home for a holiday with his relatives.

But there was also a grim side to the operations in Aden. We'd got orders for another ambush north of Habilayn. This would follow the same general pattern as previous jobs – we'd infiltrate into a position by night, lie-up, and then 19 Troop would put in an ambush on a track while we gave them top-cover from the ridge line. Fairly straightforward.

We got a drop-off from the Stalwarts and began the march in. It was the usual hard bash along narrow tracks strewn with fist- and head-sized rocks as we climbed slowly in the dark, laden with heavy rucksacks, radios and weapons. When we reached the ridge line, we shook out into our positions almost unconsciously, seeking the widest possible view over the ambush area below.

It's a strange feature of the SAS that even though the soldiers are trained to the highest possible level of skill, they come from all kinds of different military backgrounds, and someone from, say, the Royal Electrical and Mechanical Engineers isn't necessarily going to have the same degree of tactical know-how as someone who's been in the Paras for five years. In this case the troop commander down below – who was a Para – made the odd decision to split his ambush. This meant that some of the guys in the killer groups couldn't see what was happening in the other part of the ambush: a risky situation.

It so happened that Yogi in 19 Troop was an ex-Gunner who'd never been in the infantry. Lying in his position on the right of the ambush he felt the need for a piss, but instead of crawling back to the rear of the position to do it – which is what he would have done if he'd come from an infantry background and had had a hard-arse sergeant to bash him round the head for being stupid – he went forward to the edge of the killing zone.

Yogi was kneeling up taking his piss when the enemy turned up. The boys on the left side of the position, not being able to see Yogi, initiated the ambush while he was still in the killing zone, and a devastating crossfire developed as the guerrillas returned fire in greater numbers than anyone expected.

From above we could see that all hell was let loose, but the situation was too confused for us to join in and we could only watch in frustration as the firefight developed. Inevitably, word came over the VHF set that 19 Troop had a man down, Yogi, and needed a medic fast.

The first to get to him was one of 19 Troop's medics, Ray Allam. Yogi was soaked in his own blood, lying in a semi-foetal position amongst the rocks, as if trying to hug himself. He'd been hit maybe five or six times but he was still conscious, and in dreadful pain.

Ray gently began to examine him, taking in the big exit wounds from the high-velocity bullets that had ripped through his body.

'Where does it hurt, mate?'

'Jesus! My arms are killing me . . .' Yogi could just about manage a whisper. This was bad: it meant that his lungs had been lacerated by the bullets passing through his torso.

'Don't worry, mate, this'll sort you out.' Yogi had two army-issue syrettes of morphine on a cord round his neck, along with his dog-tags. The medic carefully cut them free and injected the first one into Yogi's thigh. In theory you should never use morphine for wounds to the head and torso – it depresses the respiratory system at a time when your body needs all the help it can get – but it was obvious that Yogi wasn't going to make it, and the decision was taken that he should go as quickly and in as little pain as possible.

As the drug took effect, Yogi sighed and began to breathe slightly easier. 'Thanks, mate . . . thanks.'

We'd called for a helicopter Casevac, but there was no way it would make it in time, so for twenty minutes the big tough SAS medic held his friend's hand and stroked his forehead as he died.

Then a message came to leave the body and make for the emergency RV.

'It's not a body, it's Yogi,' the troop signaller replied, 'and we're bringing him out with us.'

The troop put together a makeshift stretcher and carried him for the two hours it took to reach the emergency RV.

Not long after that 16 Troop, the free-fallers, got a break from operations and went parachuting from Scout helicopters for a few days. At the end of the training, the pilot asked whether anyone fancied going on an internal night-time security patrol with him. The idea was that the helicopter would fly over dodgy areas at altitude, drop powerful parachute flares then fly around underneath them, seeing if they could spot any baddies. A couple of the lads fancied a 'cabby' around in the helicopter but there was only space for one and Taff Iles won.

Later that evening 16 Troop were sitting around having a couple of beers with some of the other aircrew when a message came through: the helicopter had crashed in a nearby wadi.

A Wessex was quickly organized to fly 16 Troop out to the scene of the crash, but when they saw it, they immediately feared the worst. It seemed that the rotors had touched the walls of the wadi and the helicopter had smashed into the rockface about half way down, where the wreckage was still precariously poised. The Wessex pilot immediately agreed to take a group up to the wreck to check for any survivors, and he held his helicopter in a steady hover, the rotors just eighteen inches away from the rockface, whilst a team from the troop roped down. As they feared, the pilot and the crewman, a REME fitter, were both dead, and so was Taff.

A few days later, a funeral was held in the cemetery at Silent Valley for all three, and Taff's elderly father was flown out from Wales to attend. As his son's coffin was lowered into his grave, he stood proud and still, his black civilian suit a striking contrast to our khaki drills. A piper played a lament, and then Taff's dad produced an ordinary jam jar from his pocket. In the silence we could hear him unscrewing the tin lid. The jar was filled with rich, dark soil, and he poured it over the wooden coffin.

'I've brought some of home for you, son,' he said.

Our second tour lasted about three months in all. Mobility Troop hung around in Aden for several weeks after the main body of the squadron had gone, in the hope of carrying out a Land Rover-based task between Aden and the mountains, but nothing came of it because most of the troop had been poached to bodyguard Foreign Office personnel and other political types. Soon after we left, the Federal National Guard mutinied, killing and wounding a number of British troops before they were suppressed, and in the last months of the British presence, the whole place became almost ungovernable as the various local factions fought it out with each other. For my part, I was happy to leave, and with the benefit of hindsight, I can only wonder why on earth we expended so much effort and so many lives on a place that we were abandoning anyway. It makes no sense to me.

CHAPTER SIX

About a year after we returned from Aden, things started to change. I'd been in the Regiment for five years now, I'd earned my first stripe and I was accepted by the hierarchy, even if they didn't necessarily share my sense of humour. In some ways I felt it was time to move on within the regimental system. In part this was prompted by the departure of Lofty from the troop. He'd reached that 'up or out' stage of his career and went off to 23 SAS – the TA Regiment – as a sergeant major. Lofty's successor as 18 Troop staff sergeant was someone that I didn't get on with at all – an ex-REME mechanic, as it happens – so I made the decision to move sideways into 16 Troop and become a free-faller.

I'm not going to dwell on free-fall. I did it for a couple of years and even made it on to the Regimental free-fall team which, astonishingly enough in the ultra-secret SAS, used to do the occasional display at local fêtes and fairs. But the only reason I was able to do it was because I was near comatose with fright. It is a tremendous thrill to leap out into the slipstream of an aircraft at 20,000 feet and free-fall down to 3,000 feet or so at 120 miles per hour, but you've only got to see the mess when something goes badly wrong to realize how dangerous it is. During the second part of my free-fall training, which was conducted down at the French parachute school at Pau near the Pyrenees, I bought myself a pair of special jump-boots, which had extra thick, spongy, padded soles. Some time later, 16 Troop were doing a jump on Salisbury Plain for the BBC *Tomorrow's World* programme and one of the lads – Pat Martin – asked to borrow the boots. I lent them to him and off he went.

It was a routine jump and shouldn't have been a problem, but for some reason Pat's main canopy didn't open properly and when he deployed his reserve, it caught up on his oxygen bottle then tangled up with the remains of his main 'chute. Someone gave me the boots back but I never wore them again.

There were other deaths at this time. Alan Lonney, who'd come from 2 Para with me, was killed when a Pink Panther rolled over on a training rally in the Hereford area; and Ron Adey died of cerebral malaria during Christmas leave, having gone home thinking he'd got a touch of flu.

These sad events, and a quiet year or so of training in 16 Troop – it was a relatively quiet time for the Regiment as a whole – were followed by a real change as I moved out of D Squadron. The biggest problem that the Regiment had was that it was always under strength. When I'd joined there were just two squadrons, adding up to about a hundred operational SAS men in total, but as I was finishing my training B Squadron was being established, which brought the numbers up.

In the mid-1960s we'd had two operational theatres running simultaneously, Aden and Borneo, and the stress had begun to tell. For one thing, there was relatively little time to unwind between operational tours because you'd no sooner got back from one than you had to start build-up training for the next. Taken in combination with the fact that we weren't very well paid, and that we were always being dragged away from home to do something or other, it wasn't surprising that we were all under a certain amount of stress.

One attempt to solve this had been the creation, in 1967, of G Squadron. The experience of establishing B Squadron had shown that to get an operational squadron up and running from scratch was hard work and took a long time. G Squadron was an attempt to circumvent this. Out in Borneo, we'd had various organizations working for us under the command of the SAS 'theatre' headquarters. These had included the Australian and New Zealand SAS contingents, the Border Scouts, who were locally raised and trained tribesmen, the Parachute Regiment squadron and the Guards Independent Parachute Company. The Aussies and the Kiwis had done pretty much the same job as us, the Border Scouts were doing their own thing anyway, but the Para and Guards squadrons had a sort of hybrid role. They did long patrols in the jungle, but their operations weren't mounted on quite the same basis as ours.

Nevertheless, when it was decided to found a new squadron for 22 SAS we looked to people who had worked with us in the past, and the nucleus of the squadron was created by simply taking fifteen volunteers from the Guards Parachute Company, giving them nice new berets with winged dagger badges, and telling them that they were now members of G Squadron, 22 SAS. It's fair to say that there was a certain amount of outrage in the Regiment over this decision. It wasn't that they weren't good soldiers – almost all of them were – but so were a lot of lads who'd failed selection over the years. It was the principle rather than the people.

But the formation of G Squadron still wasn't enough to keep pace with the demands that were placed on the

Regiment by operations and by our other commitments, so it was therefore decided to set up an additional squadron of territorials and reservists who could be called upon in time of war to supplement the regular squadrons: R Squadron.*

The idea was that we'd recruit a combination of ex-members of the Regiment who wanted to carry on doing some training after they'd left the Army, ex-members of other army units, as well as local Hereford lads who fancied training with what, after all, was their local regiment. They would then do the proper selection course, followed by continuation, combat survival and parachute training as and when they could fit it in (obviously, the people who'd already been in the Regiment didn't have to bother with this). At the end of this they would be badged and would then do most of their training with regular squadrons on exercises.

The regular staff for R Squadron was small: an OC, a sergeant major, a storeman, a clerk and me, the PSI or permanent staff instructor, and temporarily promoted to sergeant. My job was to ensure that the volunteers were fit enough to turn up for selection, to organize courses for them and instruct them in the basics, making sure that they weren't going to let the squadrons down, and keep an eye on them all on a day-to-day basis.

R Squadron shouldn't be confused with the two territorial SAS regiments, 21 and 23. 21 SAS was set up after the Second World War and is the direct successor to the wartime SAS of David Stirling and Co. Their original role was the classic jeep-mounted long-range reconnaissance and behind-the-lines raiding that had evolved as the SAS task in the western desert and northern Europe, before eventually becoming

---

* Now renamed, somewhat pretentiously, 'L Detachment', in honour of the original SAS unit set up in 1941 by David Stirling.

the Corps Patrol Unit for 1st British Corps in Germany. 23 SAS had also started life as a successor unit to a Second World War organization, in their case MI9, which fixed evasion lines for downed aircrew and stranded soldiers. Like 21 SAS they had also slowly evolved into a part of the CPU. Both regiments wore the SAS badge and were part of the SAS family, but they had their own job and their own selection and training procedures. R Squadron was a part of 22 SAS and had to cut the mustard.

But despite this, it wasn't a job that I was hugely enthusiastic about. After a couple of years off operations I was feeling the call of the wild: I wanted to get a Bergen on my back, get overseas and do my job. Too much sitting around in Hereford makes Pete a dull boy. And so it came to pass, at the beginning of 1971, that I swapped jobs with Jimmy Collins.

Jimmy was in 6 Troop, B Squadron: Boats. When I'd first joined the Regiment I'd been in Boats. I'd done the course – diving, canoeing, rigid raiders and so on – and I'd hated it. But B Squadron were off to Malaya for Operation Pensnet. Hmmm, at the end of the day there was no choice: I wanted to get out and about again, and if that meant going to a Boat Troop, I was prepared to do it.

Malaya was pretty straightforward. We did three weeks' training before moving into Brinchang in the Cameron Highland for a jungle survival and patrolling exercise/operation. Even then, ten years after the end of the Malayan Emergency, there were still tiny groups of Communist terrorists hanging around in remote parts of the country and our presence was partly, at least, to act as a deterrent against any renewed activity on their part, particularly as the Vietnam War was now at its height.

But we were only a few weeks into the exercise when we received a signal: training was cancelled and we were to return to Hereford to begin build-up training for a new operational deployment. We were to be sent to the province of Dhofar in the south of the Sultanate of Muscat and Oman, directly adjoining, as it happens, the former Aden Protectorate, now renamed the People's Democratic Republic of Yemen. The task was named Operation Storm.

Oddly enough, it wasn't the first time that the Regiment had operated in Oman (as the country is usually called). In 1958 when the Malayan Emergency had been winding down and the Regiment was preparing to leave to come to Britain for the first time – and was facing an uncertain future – a job had come up in Oman that had saved 22 SAS's bacon.

Oman is a thinly populated country, which occupies about 1300 miles of the eastern coastline of the Arabian peninsula, and features a coastal strip, mountainous inland regions and part of the desert known as the Empty Quarter. Most of the people live in the towns and ports of the coastal strip. The traditionalist tribes live in the mountainous inland areas, notably the plateau of Jebel Akhdar in the north and in the mountains of Dhofar to the south.

Historically Oman, which also at times controlled the island of Zanzibar and parts of the coast of East Africa, was ruled by a religious imam who combined spiritual with secular authority – a bit like the ayatollahs in Iran – but in the eighteenth century the two roles were split and the country came under the authority of a sultan based in the port of Muscat. In the early nineteenth century Britain began to develop a relationship with the Sultan of Oman, mainly because it was anxious to bring an end to the slave trade in the Arabian peninsula, but also because of the country's relative closeness to British India.

The relationship was developed in the second part of the nineteenth century when the Sultan was forced to call on the

British to help him put down a rebellion by angry funda-mentalist tribesmen from the interior of the country. This created a pattern for, effectively, the next seventy-five years: the coastal-based Sultan ruled with the backing of British military force and control of the ports. The relationship was formalized in 1920 with a treaty between the inland tribes and the Sultan, which kept the peace until 1954.

The cause of the rebellion that ultimately led to the deployment of 22 SAS in the Oman was the death in 1954 of the Imam who had negotiated the 1920 treaty. Leaders of the influential Bani Riyam and Bani Hinya tribes conspired to have a young Bani Hinya man, Ghalib ibn Ali, elected as his successor. Having achieved this, the new Imam's brother, Talib, used his authority to attack a group of oil prospectors working in a neighbouring tribe's area. This in turn provoked a reaction from the Sultan's army, which forced the new Imam and his Bani Riyam allies to take refuge in their tribal villages, and which led Talib to leave for Saudi Arabia where he hoped to raise and arm a force of expatriate Omanis.

The rebellion began at an interesting time in Arab history. In Egypt Gamel Abdul Nasser had seized power and was attempting to reassert Egyptian control over the country, which had been virtually occupied by Britain for many years. At the same time the huge wealth created by oil deposits in the Gulf states was giving the Arabs a level of influence they had not enjoyed since the time of the Crusades. As a result it was a good opportunity for Talib to seek help to get rid of a sultan he could smear as a puppet of the British. When he returned to the Jebel Akhdar in June 1957 with considerable quantities of weapons, some Saudi-trained Omanis and the support of the two tribes, he quickly seized control of the central part of Oman and declared its independence from the Sultan.

Although Talib's rebellion was not widely supported outside the Bani Riyam and Bani Hinya tribes, he was in a strong military position because of his control of the Jebel Akhdar. The massive plateau effectively controlled the land routes inland from Muscat and was supposedly impregnable to attack by land forces. Once again, the Sultan called on the British for assistance.

In reality, the military problem presented by the rebellion was not that great. Talib's force of Saudi-trained soldiers numbered no more than five hundred and would be no match for a British infantry battalion, for example, provided one could be got on to the plateau. The real problem was political: by the time that Britain came to consider committing regular forces to resolve the situation we'd had the Suez fiasco and British prestige was at an all-time low amongst the Arab states. Sending in regular British Army units or formations for long-term operations in any part of Arabia which wasn't actually a part of the British Empire (unlike Aden) would be met with enormous hostility and suspicion and probably denounced in the UN. Instead, in 1957 an infantry brigade was briefly deployed from Kenya to seize low-lying areas held by the rebels, and a number of British officers and NCOs were attached to the Sultan's forces to 'stiffen' them with experienced leadership and more up-to-date tactics as they attempted to enforce a blockade of the Jebel Akhdar, where Talib's forces had scuttled after the arrival of the British brigade. At the same time RAF squadrons based in the region began a campaign of bombing against suspected rebel bases.

In the meantime, Major Frank Kitson, a staff officer working in the Military Operations branch of the Ministry of Defence, was sent to study the problem with a view to finding a long-term solution and had come to the conclusion that a fairly small-scale special operation could be mounted with a reasonable chance of success. He wanted to use bribery to discover when groups of rebels were coming off the plateau, and to mount ambushes to capture as many as possible. He then reckoned that sufficient of these people could be 'turned' to form a pseudo-rebel team that might be able to bluff the pickets at the pass onto the Jebel, or at least to get close enough to overpower them, which would allow a larger infantry force to get up there and hunt down the rebels.

This idea was accepted by the powers-that-be and a trawl began for personnel suitable to carry out Kitson's plan. While this was going on, some bright spark suggested that the ideal solution was to send an SAS squadron and the call went out to Malaya for one.

Not long after the initial recces, D Squadron flew out from Malaya on a roundabout trip that took them via Ceylon and Aden as a deception, and after a week to acclimatize to the conditions, began a campaign of aggressive patrolling around the foot of the Jebel, in an attempt to find a way up. Not long after this, they found one – an unguarded and long-forgotten track – and soon after this the first SAS patrols – including a young, fresh-faced and cherubic Lofty Large, rosy-cheeked with excitement – had established themselves on the plateau.

This unforeseen success led the headshed to bring out A Squadron as well, and not more than six weeks later it was all over: the rebels had fled or been killed, their weapons captured, and the Jebel Akhdar was firmly under the control of the Sultan's government.

The most important effect of the Jebel Akhdar campaign, which made no impression in the UK at all, was that it ensured the survival of the Regiment by showing that 22 SAS was more than just a specialist jungle warfare unit, but it also gave the Regiment a track record in Arabia, which was to stand us in good stead in later years.

The roots of the second rebellion that we got involved in lay in several different areas of Omani life. The Sultan was an old guy called Sai'id bin Taimur (the same man who was ruling the country during the Jebel Akhdar revolt) and to describe him as a feudal and autocratic despot would be somewhat mild. Although he was apparently a charming and kindly individual, he had little understanding of the modern world and was fearful of its intrusion into his kingdom. Oil had been discovered in Oman in the early 1960s, making it potentially very wealthy, but Sultan Sai'id was unwilling to borrow money to modernize the country and most of it was like something out of the Middle Ages. This situation was compounded by Sai'id's belief that in preventing modernization he would be able to maintain control of the country. Fearful that modern education – even modern techniques of agriculture – might serve as a focus for dissent, he ruthlessly used his armed forces, which were still largely composed of British officers on loan and 'contract' service (mercenaries, in other words), and Baluchis from Pakistan, to suppress any signs of development, even going to the extent of concreting over newly dug wells and destroying crops.

Not unnaturally this pissed the people off. They were perfectly capable of discovering how the world was changing outside their own borders, and anyway they were now being subjected to a stream of propaganda from the Communist People's Democratic Republic of Yemen, as well as from Cairo, Baghdad and other centres of Arab nationalism. In any case, although the Sultan was, theoretically, an absolute monarch, in practice his freedom of action had always been partly circumscribed by the tribal chiefs of the interior, who traditionally regarded him as an effete plainsman. Not surprising, then, that rebellion was breaking out throughout Oman within two years of our victory on the Jebel Akhdar and that, despite the best efforts of the Sultan's Armed Forces (SAF), it was growing stronger all the time.

But, having said that, the discontent of a gaggle of traditionally rebellious mountain tribesmen in a feudal backwater on the Arabian peninsula would have been of little interest, were it not for the strategically vital position of Oman at the mouth of the Persian Gulf. Oil from Kuwait, Iraq, Iran and Saudi Arabia was transported in vast quantities through the narrow Straits of Hormuz, which divide Oman from Iran, and an unfriendly government would theoretically possess a stranglehold on a considerable proportion of the world's oil supply. Not surprisingly, a number of parties had a strong interest in the outcome of the Dhofari rebellion and both Soviet and Chinese aid was making its way to the rebel factions in the mountains.

We began to get involved again when Johnny Watts, the commanding officer, made a covert tour of the Gulf travelling as Mr Smith. From his visit to Oman and from his previous knowledge of the country (he had commanded D Squadron during the Jebel Akhdar campaign), he recognized that a number of urgent measures needed to be taken in order for the increasingly beleaguered Sultan's armed forces to get a grip on the situation. Principal amongst these was a need to begin to win over the 'hearts and minds' of the Dhofaris rather than just punishing them, but the Sultan proved impervious to persuasion on this front. Johnny came marching home again, knowing that it was likely we were going to have to get involved, but not knowing when.

Just four months after his quiet visit to Oman – and possibly partly as a result of it – the situation changed drastically. On 23 July 1970 Sultan Sai'id was deposed in a *coup d'état*, almost certainly engineered by MI6, and replaced by his son Qaboos, who had been partly educated in Britain, had trained at Sandhurst, and had served in a British Army regiment. He had been under virtual house arrest after returning to Oman. The way was now clear for a radical policy change.

One of the first things the Regiment did was to send in a bodyguard team to look after Qaboos and to make sure that nobody did to him what he'd done to his dear old dad. Then it was on to proper operations. The first people in were G Squadron, who did an operation right up in the north of the country, on the Musandam Peninsula where Iraqi special forces were supposedly subverting the local tribes. This information turned out to be complete cobblers, but this was only discovered after Paul Reddy, from G Squadron Air Troop, had whistled in from 12,000 feet on an operational free-fall. Meanwhile, Keith Farnes, who was B Squadron's commander, had led a recce to assess the prospects for a counter-insurgency campaign in Dhofar and Johnny Watts himself had set to work on what he hoped was going to be a winning strategy.

To a very large extent the main cause of Dhofari unrest had been removed when Qaboos took power from his father. A lot of the rebels, who were simply traditionalists who didn't like being oppressed by the Sultan and his armed forces, began to drift back to areas under the new Sultan's control in the months which followed. This actually served to highlight a division amongst the rebels between a hard core of Communists and the more traditionally minded tribesmen who had simply baulked at the Sultan's repressive regime. Some Dhofaris were now beginning to suffer at the hands of the anti-Islamic Communists who behaved with typical arrogance in the areas under their control. Nevertheless there were many areas of policy in which rapid changes had to be made if the whole of Dhofar wasn't going to fall under Communist domination. Johnny Watts came up with a five-point plan to bring the situation under control. He argued that the Regiment should provide or facilitate:

1. An intelligence cell.
2. An information team.
3. A medical officer supported by SAS medics.
4. A veterinary officer.
5. When possible, the raising of Dhofari soldiers to fight for the Sultan.

These five fronts, as they were called, became the basis for most SAS operations conducted as part of Operation Storm.

But the big problem in the early days of the campaign was getting out on the Jebel where it mattered. The Sultan's armed forces had spent so long getting their arses kicked by the Adoo* that they'd developed what we called *jebelitis* – they spent as little time as possible out on the Jebel, often staying for only twenty-four hours or less – and this was having serious negative effects on the campaign. One factor in warfare – psychological warfare particularly – which is often overlooked by us westerners is 'face'. In many cultures, it's almost as bad to suffer loss of face as it is to be physically defeated. Even after the Sultan's armed forces had changed their *modus operandi* and switched to attempting to win the hearts and minds of the Dhofaris, every time they left the Jebel with their tails between their legs, they lost face in the eyes of the people they were trying to win over. Our job was to get on to the Jebel and stay there.

* The rebels.

So Operation Pensnet came to an end and we hurried back
to Hereford to begin our pre-deployment training for Oman.
The annoyance of this rapid change of plan – a fast-ball, as
it's referred to in the army – was lessened somewhat by the
twenty flagons of army-issue rum that Arthur Eggleston, the
squadron quartermaster sergeant, had smuggled back with
us. As we started the round of weapon training, navigation
and so on, a small team under Ken Borthwick and Mal Parry
headed straight out to the SAS base at Um al Gwarif, close to
the Dhofari capital at Salalah, to act as advance party for the
squadron.

With our work-up complete, and under the command of a
new boss, Major 'Duke' Pirie, we boarded C-130s at Lyneham
for the flight out to Oman. We flew directly into Salalah, and
after a couple of hours' stretching our legs and unloading the
Hercules, we all piled aboard two SAF Caribou short take-off
and landing transports, with a motley selection of Arabs and
their goats and chickens, for the hop to a small airfield at the
foot of the Jebel codenamed 'Midway'.

At Midway, we had an overnight stop, sleeping out in the
open. Then we piled aboard a convoy of open-backed three-
ton trucks and began a laborious eight-hour drive up a wadi
bed to an RV. There we met up with our advance party and
the other elements who were taking part in the operation –
now named Operation Jaguar. Apart from ourselves, we also
had G Squadron, who had been out in Oman for some time,
conducting recces, two companies of SAF Baluchis, and five
Firqat units all under the command of Johnny Watts.

Now the 'Firks' were an interesting bunch because almost
all of them were former members of the Adoo who had changed
sides. They were one of the first elements of Watts's five fronts
that got going and they were largely trained and led by the
SAS, under the cover of the 'British Army Training Team'.

When they had surrendered, they were welcomed back into the fold, they weren't mistreated, they were paid for turning in their weapons, and they were gently debriefed about their experiences with the Adoo. Although their job was supposedly to defend their tribal areas, their mere existence was a potent weapon in the intelligence and psychological war against the Communists, because it gave the lie to the propaganda that prisoners were routinely abused and killed and that the Dhofaris could not trust the government. They were also a force in which Islam was tolerated and even encouraged.

What the Firqats weren't so good at was fighting. They were certainly brave and they knew the terrain very well but, at the end of the day, they lacked the discipline of a well-drilled military force, which put them at a disadvantage in the kind of broken-up running battle we were preparing to fight.

We spent about two days getting ourselves acclimatized to the heat and conditions, sending out patrols to look over our anticipated routes onto the Jebel and getting briefed on the plan. This was pretty straightforward: the force was to be broken down into two groups, West and East, which would then climb up to the plateau and, in effect, advance to contact, hitting the Adoo with everything we had. The difference between this and previous operations was that this time we were going to stay for good.

The briefing from the G Squadron recce was that we would be on the Jebel in approximately four hours, but that we would reach a waterhole in two. It occurred to me that this was probably optimistic: I'd heard similar things in Aden. Even though it would add a considerable weight to my Bergen, I went off and filled a gallon can to take with me. Ted Stafford saw me doing this and started to take the piss, but I shrugged it off.

'Ted, don't forget that when G Squadron did their recces, they were in light-order four-man patrols. There's nearly a battalion of us, speaking at least three languages. It's going to take us four hours to leave here, let alone get on the Jebel.'

'Bollocks, Scholey.'

Well, it didn't bother me and I was the one with the extra weight after all.

At about 1830, in the cool of the evening, we set off on one of the hardest marches I've ever done. I was a member of one of the mortar teams with West group, but at that stage we didn't have the mortars with us because they were too heavy to manpack over long distances, so I was with the guys, just plodding along at the back. After about six hours' climbing, we halted for a rest on an open area while Mal Parry went forward with Cappy to recce the next phase of our route. By this time everyone was so chin-strapped that they just flopped to the deck and lay there. I had to go round telling them to get themselves shaken out into all-round defence while we waited for Mal to return. Funnily enough, and it's a point worth making, nobody resented me telling them to do this. In some units I'd have got an earful if I'd started making this sort of suggestion when everyone was shagged out, but in that situation I was correct and every-one accepted it, even if it did mean a certain amount of inconvenience.

Mal and Cappy got back from their recce looking completely shattered, having run out of water. I passed them a full bottle and told them to share it.

'We can't take this, Pete. What about you?'

'I brought a gallon with me from Aden.'

Cappy had been in Aden with me and managed a laugh, and then we got the lads up and began to trudge onwards.

We hadn't got very far when word came up the column. 'Slow down, slow down! Ginge Rees has dropped dead!'

'WHAT?'

'Doc McLuskey's giving him the suck of life . . .'

Poor old Ginge was carrying well over a hundred pounds of kit and combined with the heat, the humidity and the climb, he'd keeled over and appeared, to all intents and purposes, to have died. In fact it was a severe case of heat exhaustion and after treatment, his kit was distributed amongst the squadron and he carried on. Talk about guts!

We kept climbing, and just over fifteen hours after leaving the drop-off point, made it to the plateau, though by now the entire force was strung out down the mountain in a great long line. From the top of the escarpment, our B Squadron positions were about a thousand metres across an area of flat open ground and I soon made it over there, dropping off my Bergen and watching as the rest of the squadron trudged into the position.

I was talking to two of the young troop commanders, Mike Kealy, a captain from the Royal Fusiliers and Derek Dale, a flight lieutenant from the RAF Regiment, who was in command of my mortar team. As we stood there, I saw Ted Stafford limping slowly along in the distance, bowed under the weight of his gear, so I nipped out and took his Bergen off him and brought it in. When I got back, Boss Kealy blinked at me through his little gold-rimmed glasses and said, 'That was very nice of you, Peter.'

'I was taught that in the Gunners, boss. It's called team spirit.'

By now the rest of my mortar group had arrived and were slumped down, poleaxed by exhaustion and dehydration. I got the gallon can out and made a brew of tea and we sat there and drank it as we tried to recover enough energy to get on with our tasks. Apart from me and Derek, there were four of us in the team: Topper Brown, Charlie Cook, Jakey Ovendon and Frenchy Williams; they were all surprised I had any water left.

'Where'd you get that, Pete?'

'Like I said, I brought it from Aden.'

We secured the flat ground, an old SAF airstrip codenamed 'Lympne', and soon after the helicopters began to arrive, bringing in food, water and ammunition. First go at this went to the Firks who tended to need a bit of jollying along (and also because a lot of them had thrown away their rations rather than carry them up the hill) and we didn't get ours before about four in the afternoon.

By now we were in a position to make an assessment of the kind of shape the squadron was in. Ted Stafford's knee was completely fucked up, and he went back down the Jebel, never to be seen again (on this operation at least) and Pete Spicer – 'the Toad' – had gone down with heat exhaustion and needed a day or so's treatment before returning to the operation. With the area secured, B Squadron were then told to concentrate at a nearby waterhole for the night.

We got to the waterhole and I immediately thought, 'Whoa! No way!' The problem was that it was a kind of steep-sided rocky crater with water in the bottom, and if we were all inside it wouldn't take much more than a couple of mortar bombs or an artillery round to really screw us up. It was at this point that the shooting started up above us, and no messing about, it was serious shit.

We were all looking about us, waiting for someone to take a lead when a round came in, pinged off some rocks, then slapped into Jakey Ovendon's leg, without breaking the skin. I reached down and picked up the twisted, spent Kalashnikov round, gave it to Jake, and said, 'Here you go mate, a souvenir for you.'

But, despite the jokes, I was worried that we hadn't reacted sensibly to the fire that was coming in and that we were still skulking down in the waterhole. Adrenaline took a hold of me and I shouted, in my best John Wayne accent, 'Come on, guys, we've gotta get to the high ground!'

There was general agreement to this suggestion and as the volume of fire began to decrease, Cappy led the squadron into a more sensible defensive position and we began to dig in for the night, not without feeling a certain amount of tension.

We'd sorted ourselves out with shallow shell-scrapes (the ground was too hard for anything deeper than a few inches) and were standing around having a brew and a chat when there was a sudden burst of fire right in amongst us. Luckily nobody was hit but the scene looked like *Bambi* when the gunshot goes off and all the little animals scamper hippity-lippity back to their holes, in our case leaving a trail of spilt tea and compo biscuits. We stood to, but the contact soon died down, leaving us in a state of uneasy peace for the rest of the night.

Next morning, Johnny Watts was with us as we formed up to begin the advance to contact in our little teams. We'd split down into action groups and support groups and the plan was to skirmish forwards through this undulating scrubland towards a place called Jibjat until we ran into the enemy, and then to take them on. As we were shaking out, Duke Perry walked over to Johnny Watts and said, 'Colonel, we've spotted some movement. What shall we do?'

'We'll go and fucking kill them!'

And we were off.

The first patrols out of Lympne were some of the most intense soldiering I've done. Apart from the fact that it was extremely hot and tiring and that we were, as usual, carrying a great deal of kit about with us, we were running into heavy contacts every time out. On the first day, as I carefully patrolled forwards with Derek, we suddenly came under intense sustained fire from an Adoo machine-gun. We both dived for cover, but I noticed that Derek had got himself into the illusory safety of a bush, as opposed to the rather more substantial rock recommended by most training manuals.

With the *crack!* of high-velocity bullets smacking all around us I peeped out to look at Derek, and using my best officer's voice told him, 'Derek, cover from view is not cover from fire.'

He gave this proposition a couple of seconds' thought – 'Fuck!' – and he scrabbled into cover with me.

But we weren't out of the woods yet. The Adoo machine-gunner was dropping bullets all round us and it was clearly time to move. A little way away, Jakey Ovenden was crouching behind a rock with a sniper's rifle, and I told him I'd cover him as he headed for a ridge a couple of hundred metres away.

Jakey set off, and as he ran, I fired a few double-taps in the direction of the enemy from my SLR. When Jakey reached cover at a little knoll near the ridgeline, I set off in the same direction jogging as fast as I could under the weight of my Bergen, belt kit and weapon, with Derek Dale close behind. As I got close to Jakey, I shouted that I would cover him on the final stretch, but as I was saying this, he shouted back, 'Scholey, don't stop, don't stop!'

I looked around ... JESUS CHRIST! The machine-gunner was tracking me and the bullets were hitting the ground just behind my feet. If I'd stopped, he'd have taken my legs off.

I shrugged off the Bergen and sprinted the last few metres past Jakey and over the ridge line where I found about ten members of G Squadron, pissing themselves laughing at me.

I had a momentary sense-of-humour failure. 'You cunts! They nearly fucking got me!'

I sank down to the ground feeling completely drained as the adrenaline left my system. As I lay there, a message came over to say that Jim Vakatalia had been hit further over, and they needed volunteers to go and help him. Old Joe Little jumped up to go and I watched as he darted out of the position.

I was still lying there recovering myself a few minutes later when I heard the sound of the Casevac chopper taking Jim out to the FST,* and I distinctly remember thinking: I really don't want to do any more of this: it's fucking dangerous!

The contact died down a bit and Jakey and Derek made it up to the ridge. Then Ned Kelly, one of the G Squadron boys, called over, in his thick Scottish accent, 'Scholey, yer gannae have tae get yer Bergen.'

I looked down to where I'd dropped it, about 150 metres away and thought, Bollocks! But it was true, I did have to go and get it. I slowly got up then wearily walked down to where it was lying and pulled it onto my shoulders. I turned about and began to trudge back to the position when *BAM-BAM-BAM-BAM-BAM-BAM!* A long burst of tracer whipped over my head. I dived to the ground, crawled a few yards and then dashed as fast as I could back up to the ridge. When I got there, the G Squadron boys were literally crying with laughter, and I looked down to see smoke coming off the barrel of Ned's gympy.

'You bastard, Kelly! Never forget, I am going to get you for that.'

* Field Surgical Team.

'Sorry, Pete, we could have sworn we saw a suspicious movement . . .'

We continued the advance until the evening, arriving at a hill with a couple of small trees at the top of it which we called, with typical imagination, Twin Trees. We dug in round here, as best we could because, being SAS, we cleverly hadn't brought our digging tools, had we? And we sat out the night as the Adoo let all hell loose at us.

While all this was going on, the East group were also in the thick of it. Steve Moores, a G Squadron sergeant, was badly wounded in an Adoo ambush and died whilst being evacuated. Steve was one of the original fifteen G Squadron members but was an excellent soldier, well-liked in the Regiment. Even Kevin Walsh, the airborne wart, got hit. He was in a position that was suddenly swept by machine-gun fire and, because he couldn't get into a sangar (because, he used to claim, they'd all filled up with officers) he took cover behind a stack of jerrycans. Unknown to him, they were all empty and he took a round up the arse fired, so Lofty Wiseman alleged, by a fat Arab TA cook on a weekend exercise.

There was something poetic, if that's the right word, about the location of Kevin's wound. As he was carried through the position to the Casevac chopper, he was telling the doctor, 'It hurts, it hurts.'

The doctor responded briskly, 'Of course it hurts: you've been shot.'

'Not that, you prat, you've left the needle from the morphine sticking in my arse.'

They got him away to the FST at Salalah where he was in a ward with a number of other wounded men, lying face down on a nice crisp hospital bed. Unfortunately, there was something really pissing him off, and it all came to a head when the Brigadier paid him a visit.

'Kevin, I'm so sorry to hear that you've been shot in the arse . . .'

'Brigadier, I've told everyone else, and now I'm going to tell you: IT IS NOT MY ARSE, IT'S MY UPPER THIGH!'

The brigadier was a bit taken aback by this, but an SAS NCO who was there visiting another of the wounded, chipped in, 'Sir, you have to remember that Kevin's arse starts at the back of his neck and ends up at his ankles.'

In the end, he got so fed up with all the jokes that he discharged himself and returned to duty.

We spent a little time at Jibjat and then pushed on to a position known as White City which was to become our firm base for the time being and where we set about establishing a proper airstrip, as well as reinforced sangars, mortar pits and all the other mod cons.

From there we began to go out on patrols every day in order to dominate and then secure the area, while those who weren't out on patrol concentrated on strengthening the position, clearing the airstrip and securing the base against persistent fierce Adoo attacks.

Construction of the airstrip was being supervised by a miserable old contract officer in the Sultan's Air Force, known as Chalky White. After we'd been at White City a few days, I heard some of the lads call him Rent-a-trench, but I couldn't think why until a couple of days later when we were unloading ammunition from a helicopter that had just flown in. As the chopper was idling, we started taking machine-gun fire from outside our perimeter and we scattered for cover. I spotted a trench out of the corner of my eye and ran to jump in it, only to be stopped by Chalky.

'How many cigarettes have you got?'

'None, I don't smoke . . .'

'Well, if you want to come in here you've got to give me two fags.'

The miserable old sod wouldn't let me get in, and despite being under heavy fire, I had to find another trench to clamber into.

The Adoo were determined not to let us walk over them and almost every patrol got into a heavy contact. Soon after we'd arrived I was sitting in a trench sharing a brew with Ken Borthwick when a patrol went out on an area clearance task. No more than a few minutes after they left they came under heavy fire, and Ken and I listened as our outlying defensive positions joined in, using GPMGs set up on fixed lines. As we sat there, listening to almost continuous fire, I said to Ken, 'They'll be getting a bit short of ammunition by now . . .'

Ken's response was, 'You're right, let's run a couple of boxes up to them.'

We each grabbed a box of 7.62mm link for the gympies and scuttled up a reverse slope towards the sound of firing. Nearing the top, a lad called Griff was crouched down over a radio set, trying to make some sense of what was happening. He radioed to Sean Scanlon, who was running the gympies, to see if he needed any help and now called over to us, 'Don't go over yet, they've still got incoming fire.'

By now the contact was slackening off and Ken decided that he wasn't too fussed by the enemy fire and carried on. I, on the other hand, decided to let discretion be the better part of valour, and opted to wait with Griff until everything had quietened down.

The contact finished but word came back: 'Ken Borthwick's been shot.'

I went up to see what had happened and found Joe Little

piggy-backing him back down the hill. Ken had taken a nearly spent round in his foot and was in a lot of pain, but wasn't actually too severely injured. He got a Casevac but there was an amusing sequel to this when the padre back in Hereford was sent to see Ken's wife to tell her what had happened. One of those grim rituals that the army has is that when a soldier becomes a casualty, an officer is sent off, in full service dress, to tell his family. Usually it would be the families officer or the adjutant, but padres also get to do their share of this work, depending on the regiment. Poor Gwen Borthwick answered the door to find the padre standing there and immediately feared the worst.

'I'm sorry, Mrs Borthwick, I'm afraid I have some bad news for you.'

'Oh, my God!'

'I'm afraid that your husband has been shot.'

'Oh, no!'

'Yes, I'm afraid that he has been shot in the right foot, but he is going to be all right.'

'Thank God for that!'

But a couple of days later the padre appeared again. 'I'm sorry, Mrs Borthwick, but I'm afraid I made a terrible mistake . . .'

'Oh, no! He's dead, isn't he?'

'No, Mrs Borthwick, but it was actually his left foot.'

'Padre.'

'Yes, Mrs Borthwick?'

'Will you just piss off?'

The Green Slime (also known as the Intelligence Corps) had now worked out that the terrorists were holed up in the Wadi Darbat, a big valley about ten kilometres from White City, and that they were filtering out to hit us virtually at will. To bring this to an end, a great scheme was hatched.

The plan involved advancing to Darbat, putting in a defensive position on the high ground and then using artillery, mortars and aircraft to push the Adoo out. We had a platoon of Firqat attached to us for the operation, and as we were approaching the top of one of the wadis, a Firqa stepped on what is known as a butterfly mine.

These horrible little things are made of plastic, which means they are difficult to detect, and are about the size of the petrol cap from your car. This means that they're easy to scatter about but hard to spot, and they have become a real menace in combat zones. This particular type of mine operates on a release switch – it doesn't go off until you step *off* it, but when it does go, it will take most of your foot and ankle with it. Fortunately, our lad noticed what it was he was standing on and had the presence of mind to keep his foot firmly down. Lucky for him, but it left him and us with a problem: how were we going to get him off it?

We gathered round him to discuss what to do next as he stood there stock still, his face pale and his eyes bugging out like organ stops. This was the first time I'd seen a Jebeli sweat. Once we'd made the decision, we watched his reactions as the Arabic linguist translated the plan to him. As the explanation continued, his eyes got wider and wider: no surprise there. With each sentence, he responded in a sort of Peter Sellers accent: 'What? Again what?'

And here's what we did. We filled four sandbags and placed them around the foot that was on the mine. We then got about 150 feet of parachute cord, tied a loop round his waist, and retreated back into cover. He was staring at us over his shoulder. It seemed to go on for ever: we explained to him that we would count from ten down to one (in Arabic of course), and on the count of 'one' a team of ten of us would haul on the cord as hard and fast as we could to pull him clear. We hoped that we would be able to jerk him off the mine quickly enough for his foot to be out of the way so that the explosion was absorbed by the sandbags.

It more or less worked. We pulled him off, he lifted in the air, the mine exploded and instead of losing a foot or leg, he lost two toes. He was relieved to be still alive.

He forgot his toes and went round thanking each one of us. Brave man.

Notwithstanding this, the operation wasn't a resounding success. As we approached the wadi, the enemy met us in strength, and we were chased most of the way back to White City in a fire and movement running battle that, almost miraculously, left us with no further casualties.

But despite the occasional setback, word was beginning to get around amongst the Dhofaris that we were on the Jebel to stay, and slowly but surely, the Jebeli people began to arrive at White City to seek our help and protection. One of the first things we did was to establish a medical centre, originally in a tent and later, as the area became more secure, in a hut. When this was done, we put the word about that medical help was available and waited to see what happened.

After a while, local Jebeli tribesmen began to drift in to see our doctor – Phil McLuskey from the Royal Army Medical Corps – and the other medically trained SAS men, including me, who would act as his assistants when we weren't patrolling. As their confidence grew, they would bring in their kinsmen who were Adoo, who would surrender their weapons, join the Firqat and take part in operations, under our leadership, against their former comrades.

Everyone who arrived at the medical centre would get a good old-fashioned army FFI (Free From Infection) inspection. The men would strip off and hold their arms above their heads whilst the doc checked for lice and other external parasites, taking a few seconds per person. On average we might attract anything from ten to twenty people each day.

One morning fifteen turned up. The first thirteen went through quite happily but the doc was unhappy with the last two. Although he had checked them over and told them that they were okay, they had refused to leave and had stood gibbering at him in Arabic, which he couldn't understand. After they had stood naked with their hands up for about five minutes, he called me in. 'Pete, what's wrong with them? I finished with them ages ago.'

'I think they want to surrender to you.'

Looking amazed he asked, 'What makes you think that?'

'I asked them when they were outside, but I thought you might have had a clue from the fact that they've got their hands up and they're both offering you their AK47s.'

'You learn something new every day out here.'

We had another laugh a couple of weeks later when a tribeswoman brought in her husband. She told the doc, through one of the lads who was an Arabic speaker, that her husband had had a headache for a day or two. After the doc had examined him, he gave the woman three aspirins and told her to bring him back if they didn't work.

Six hours later the wife returned. 'The medicine has not worked, he still has the head pains.'

'Where is your husband now?'

'He's sitting outside the tent,' she replied.

'Bring him in,' said the doc, who was only a very young chap.

In came the old Jebeli with the three tablets carefully Sellotaped to his forehead.

Along with their medical problems, the Dhofaris also

began to bring their animals to White City. Somehow or other, the system had managed to burp up an army vet who was soon installed providing routine inoculations to the cattle and goats. But what they really wanted, apart from physical protection for their animals, was the chance to get them off the Jebel so they could sell them.

By the end of October, there were more than 1400 goats at Jibjat and White City, and around 600 head of scabby old cattle, and a plan was formed for us, the SAF and one of the Firqats, the Khalid bin Walid, to escort them down to the coastal town of Taqa where they could be sold. This, of course, was easier said than done.

The cattle drive was not too much of a problem in itself, because there were enough herdsmen amongst the Firks to sort out that side of it, but what was going to be hard was protecting them from the Adoo who would suffer a major loss of face if we succeeded. The vital ground of the operation – codenamed Taurus – was a canyon through which the cattle would have to pass as they descended from the Jebel. It was ideal ambush country and if we didn't secure it, the operation would rapidly turn into a complete disaster.

The solution was for teams of Firks, Baluchis and SAS to picket the high ground, and we moved out to do so some four hours before the cattle started moving. For obvious reasons, the move would be taking place at night, so we set off at last light to give the cattle time to get sorted out and make the distance before daybreak.

We started off with Cappy in the lead, steering with the aid of an IWS, a kind of first-generation image-intensifying night-sight that sat on top of your rifle like a big telescope. In relatively easy going, we were moving quite fast and the tail-end of the convoy started to get strung out. Soon word was whispered up the column: 'Tell Bob Lawson to fuckin' slow down, we're going too fast. Pass it on.' This went all the way along the line of sweating soldiers, always double-checked to make sure it wasn't turning into some gobbledegook, until the message came back: 'Bob Lawson's at the fucking back.' This caused a moment's pause for thought: 'Well, fucking slow down anyway!'

We reached the beginning of the high ground and decided that we would send a platoon of Firks up to pioneer the route, together with Mal Parry's action group. They set off, and before too long, all hell was let loose as they walked straight into a group of Adoo. There were bullets flying everywhere as Mal's gang returned fire, and the rest of us took cover against the risk of being hit by stray rounds and ricochets.

I now found myself amongst Jimmy Joint's action group as he started to give a briefing.

'Listen, lads, if we follow up behind Mal and there's Adoo on the other side of the canyon, we are going to get shat on. So I want us to go up onto the high ground on the other side and clear that as well while Mal sorts out this lot.'

I said to Jimmy, 'I don't know where my lot are. I'll come up with you if you don't mind.'

'Sure, Pete, the more the merrier.'

We moved off in single file until we reached the brow of the hill, then Jimmy told us: 'Right, lads, we'll move into extended line, like we do in the Paras. If we hit an enemy position, we'll assault straight through, okay?'

We all nodded and made fierce noises, but in the back of my mind there was a nagging thought: There's only about ten of us, we could get into some serious shit here!

We set off, patrolling purposefully forwards, but as we crested the high ground, Jimmy passed the word: 'Stop, stop!' We gathered in for an update and he told us that we were to return and rejoin Mal's group as there were no enemy on our side of the wadi and they had several casualties to deal with. We made our way quickly back, but stalled as we approached Mal because the Firk who was acting as our lead scout wouldn't go into the position because he was scared of being shot. We swapped him over and rejoined Mal to find that 'Connie' Francis and two or three Firks had been hit during their contact.

Poor Connie, he'd taken a machine-gun round in the back that had made a hell of a mess, and Mal had already used up eight or nine field dressings in an attempt to staunch the bleeding. I treated the Firks, who had relatively minor injuries, and then got on with Connie. We didn't have a stretcher with us, but I had a sleeping-bag in my Bergen and I jogged back to where I'd dropped it so that we could use it to carry Connie back to cover. We gently moved him onto the sleeping-bag and then six of us carried him back to a sort of dry stone-walled corral where we could keep him sheltered until the morning.

He was incredibly brave. He lay there the rest of the night with Bob Lawson stroking his forehead and holding his hand, hardly uttering a sound even though he must have been in a good deal of pain. In the early light of dawn, we got a message to say that the Casevac chopper was coming in but Connie was going into shock, and was convinced he was about to die.

'Bob, I'm going now, I'm going . . .'

'Aye, you're right. You're going in this fucking chopper down to Salalah.'

Which he did, and where the FST were almost miraculously able to save his life.

With all the excitement surrounding the contact and Connie, I somehow managed to miss all the cows going through, but go through they did, and safely on to Taqa where they were sold to the great profit of the Dhofaris and the intense annoyance of the rebels.

We got back to White City and resumed work on the position as the Adoo continued to probe our defences. By now we had the mortars properly set up, together with all the world's supply of ammunition, and this gave us the opportunity to conduct a few unconventional shoots. One regular event was the dawn chorus of Adoo mortars, which fired into the base at around the same time every morning. It occurred to me that it might be possible to disrupt this if we set up for a pre-emptive shoot into the enemy's firing areas at the same time. We got everything ready, with the ranges worked out, bearings taken and ammunition prepared, and I dropped the first bomb down the tube of the mortar.

There was the usual metallic sliding sound, followed by the cough of the propellant igniting. Then a strange, dream-like sensation came over me. Everything went quiet and for a few seconds I couldn't think what had happened – then I realized that the mortar bomb had detonated as it left the barrel.

It was a high-explosive bomb with a lethal fragmentation radius of sixty metres. My head was maybe two metres from the centre of the explosion. I thought: That's it then, I'm dead and I'm a ghost. Then I could hear someone shouting 'Medic! Medic!' and it began to dawn on me, I'm still alive! I felt over myself with mounting disbelief: I'm not even wounded. I can't explain it to this day.

But both Jim Penny and Jock Phillips had been hit by shrapnel from the blast and, groggy as I was, I went over to assist Doc McLuskey as he treated them. Jock had taken a big chunk of shrapnel in the leg and a helicopter had been called up to take him to the FST. As we carried him on a stretcher across to the HLS, we began to receive incoming mortar fire and as shrapnel began to spatter around us, I told the lads, 'Right, we'll put the stretcher down there by those burmails* and get into cover.'

Jock wasn't too happy about this. 'What are ye talking about? You cannae leave a wounded man.'

'Don't worry, Jock, you'll be perfectly all right.'

'What are ye saying, you bastard? Don't fuckin' leave me here! Those burmails are full of avgas.† What if they get hit?'

'Well, then, I'll treat you for burns.'

'Scholey, you cunt!'

He was perfectly safe, of course, from pretty well everything but a direct hit so we left him there until the firing stopped and we could load him aboard the Jet Ranger, which flew him on out to the FST.

We continued to consolidate our position on the Jebel for the next four months. We averaged about two or three contacts a day and the Adoo continued to hit us whenever they could. In one mortar shoot I conducted, with Steve Fraser out spotting from high ground, we managed to get a direct hit with our second round on a small gang of Adoo, causing several secondary explosions. Word later filtered back via the Firks that we'd actually taken out a complete Adoo section of eight men, which wasn't bad for a day's work. On the other hand, one patrol ran into an ambush, and in the course of a section attack, led by the CO, but also including the second-in-command and the RSM, Chris Loid took a round in the head and died the next day after evacuation to the FST.

We continued to have a few laughs as well, though, if only

---

* *Burmail* is the local word for large gasoline canisters, derived from 'Burmah Oil' which was painted on many of them.
† Aviation fuel.

to keep sane. We'd done a two-day patrol, which had entailed us building a small defensive position, and when we were leaving to return to White City, the drill was to blow it up so that it couldn't be used by the enemy. One of my lads, Topper Brown, was mad keen to get involved in everything and he volunteered to place the charges and do the demolition on our sangars. He did his stuff while we retired to a safe distance. He soon came scampering up saying that the charges would blow in about three minutes.

Three minutes passed and nothing happened, then four, then five. Kevin was back with us after his 'upper thigh' wound and he started quipping, 'Looks like you've fucked up, Top. Let's have a look.'

We raised our heads to see what was going on and spotted a tall skinny Arab herdsman, complete with flock of goats, poking around the sangars with his long shepherd's crook. We were trying to win the Jebelis' hearts and minds, not blow them apart.

'Top, if that lot goes up, you'll be for the high jump,' I told him.

'Not half as much as the fuckin' Arab,' observed Kev.

We started waving and shouting at the goatherd, who looked at us in puzzlement.

Suddenly there was a bright orange flash followed by a loud *THUD!* and a huge cloud of smoke and dust obscured our view of what was happening. Topper went white as a sheet as his career flashed before his eyes.

'Oh, fuckin' 'ell.'

Then, in a scene reminiscent of the Keystone Cops, the Arab emerged from the cloud of smoke, apparently unhurt, but shaking his fist in extreme annoyance.

Topper and I approached him and handed over rations and chocolates to try and appease him. As the goats milled round

I couldn't resist. 'So,' I said to the shepherd, 'how are the kids?'

Topper started laughing and the Arab's fist started shaking again. Definitely time to leave.

The end of the first tour saw us back in Hereford for a period of recovery before we began build-up training for our second go round. Before we'd left, we'd been talking to D Squadron's advance party, who had found it hard to believe that the intensity of the conflict had rocketed up so high in the short period between their first tour, which took place about six months before Op Jaguar, and now. Over a brew, one of them said to Kevin, 'I thought this was meant to be like the Second World War? When are we going to get our first contact, then?'

Kevin's response was straightforward. 'What time do you fuckin' fancy one? You've only got to go outside the perimeter and you'll get all the contacts you want.'

I didn't make it out on B Squadron's second tour because I'd been nominated to go off on the Infantry Jungle Warfare course in Malaya. This might seem a little strange because, first, the SAS use different jungle tactics from the infantry, and second, I guess I'd spent as much time patrolling in the jungle as any of the instructors there. A number of SAS NCOs had been sent out on the course over the years, but few had done well, not because they weren't good in the jungle, but simply because they were used to doing things differently and were unwilling to change to conform with the course requirement.

Well, that struck me as a short sighted view, to be honest. We were doing a lot of 'team tasks' by now, going overseas to train friendly armies in varying types of tactics and techniques, but one of the principal rules of this sort of work was that we taught them infantry tactics to a high standard, not SAS tactics. But if you hadn't done an infantry jungle warfare course, how could you teach infantry tactics? I put a lot of effort into the course and was rewarded with an 'A' grading and the best student award, which I was rather pleased about.

In fact, the SAS was going through one of its periodic looks at itself at about this time, with the arrival of Peter de la Billière as CO (replacing Johnny Watts). He decided that all sergeants had to go off to do the infantry 'Senior Brecon' course as a qualification for promotion. Apart from that, though, and the creation of the anti-terrorist team, some of DLB's innovations weren't quite so welcome.

One of the most outrageous was the weekly muster parade at Bradbury Lines on a Monday morning. When this was announced, there was more than a little consternation. Drill? DRILL!? The last time I'd done any serious drilling was at a Regimental funeral in the late 1960s. Lofty Large was put in charge of the burial party, which was a mistake because the last time he'd done any rifle drill was in 1957 when the army was still issued with the Lee-Enfield No. 4. The rest of us had either learnt arms drill with the SLR or the Sterling SMG, so when Lofty started giving commands like 'Slope Arms' (which weren't drill movements with the modern weapons) a certain amount of confusion ensued. Once we got that sorted out, it became a little easier and because it was the funeral of one of our comrades, we knuckled down and got it right. But a weekly parade: no thanks!

Together with drill came edicts on dress and saluting as well. By and large, most of us wore the old Second World War camouflage windproof smock when we were in the field, with olive green cotton trousers, but these too were banned in favour of the new army DPM camouflage. In barracks, we suddenly found ourselves wearing rank badges for the first time. I was determined not to let these changes go by without a protest, and having been pulled up by Keith Farnes for not saluting him, I made a point of always saluting him with my left hand. Much good it did me; he didn't notice until I told him.

One consequence of missing B Squadron's second Op Storm tour was that I wasn't around for the battle of Mirbat, one of the turning points in the Dhofar campaign. At first light on 19 July, more than 250 Adoo guerrillas of the Dhofar Liberation Front began to move towards the coastal town of Mirbat, covered by fire from both mortars and recoilless artillery. Their opposition consisted of approximately thirty Askars armed with .303 Lee-Enfield rifles, twenty-five members of the Dhofar Gendarmerie (DG) armed with Belgian FN rifles, a light machine-gun and nine members of the Regiment under Boss Kealy – eight from B Squadron, one from G Squadron, who was only there to do a stores check before his squadron took over responsibility for the town later that day. The three groups of defenders were all occupying different locations: the Askars (local soldiers) were in the town Wali's fort; the Gendarmes were in their own fort; the SAS were in their two storey BATT*-house.

Alerted by the incoming mortar fire, the SAS team stood to, expecting that it was no more than the usual 'dawn chorus' of harassing fire from the Jebel. Instead, they soon realized that they were being subjected to a sustained attack. After sending a contact report, the lads began responding using their own support weapons: an 81mm mortar and a .50

* British Army Training Team.

197

Browning heavy machine-gun; whilst Laba, a Fijian SAS corporal, made his way across 500 metres of open ground to the DG fort to operate a 25-pounder field gun which happened to be there.

The rebel attack was concentrated on the DG fort, probably with the aim of capturing the field gun. After Laba reported that he had been 'chinned' by a bullet he was joined by Tak, another Fijian, who helped him for a short period before he too was hit. By now the rebels were very close to the gun-pit and Laba was using the artillery piece as a direct fire weapon, aiming over open sights at the enemy only a few hundred metres away.

At this point Laba decided to give up on the field gun and use a 66mm mortar which was nearby. As he made his way towards it, he was shot in the neck. He died almost immediately. Tak was now on his own, wounded, and firing his SLR one-handed from the gun-pit at Adoo less than a hundred metres away.

In the BATT-house, Mike Kealy decided to take the team medic, Tommy Tobin, to the DG fort. They covered each other across the open ground but as they arrived at the gun-pit, Tobin was mortally wounded by shots to the face. Taking cover in a nearby trench, Kealy was now able to talk to Tak, but they appeared to be in an impossible situation, virtually overrun by the guerrillas attacking the fort. It was now that salvation arrived in the form of Strikemaster ground-attack aircraft of the Sultan's Air Force, which made repeated bombing and strafing runs at the guerrillas. As the momentum of the rebel attack faltered, members of G Squadron, under Alistair Morrison, arrived to reinforce the position.

It was a complete coincidence that there were two SAS squadrons in Dhofar at the time of the Mirbat battle, and even more fortunate that one of them had just completed its build-up training and was literally about to take over from the first, providing an extremely effective quick-reaction force. In the face of the stiff resistance of the Mirbat garrison, close air support and unexpected reinforcements, the Adoo had no option but to withdraw, leaving behind thirty-eight bodies. In contrast the defenders suffered nine dead, including Laba and Tobin.

As well as being a stiff military defeat, the battle of Mirbat was a major symbolic blow to the rebels, demonstrating that even in strength they were unable to overwhelm a well-organized garrison of the Sultan's forces. Although it would be incorrect to ascribe the victory entirely to the BATT, the action of Laba, Tak and Kealy at the gun-pit, supported by the mortar and machine-guns at the BATT-house, delayed the Adoo enough to ensure that they had not achieved their objectives by the time that air support (delayed by low cloud) arrived. Both the DG and the Askars in the Wali's fort fought well and deserve their share of the credit for resisting the attack but it was, in essence, an SAS victory.

The great shame was that for political reasons, only a few decorations could be awarded. Boss Kealy got a DSO, Bob Bennett an MM and Laba a posthumous Mention in Despatches. It was thought that Laba should have got the VC. Tak got the DCM. Tommy Tobin did not receive anything for his valiant action. Neither did Fuzz Hussey who was firing his 81mm mortar on the lowest charge to bring the bombs down as the enemy were so close to his own position. Nor did Roger Cole receive anything. He stood out in the open under heavy fire to put down a red smoke grenade to warn off the helicopter pilot who would surely have been shot down if he'd approached. Pete Warne was on the wall of the fort firing the Browning machine gun under heavy fire. By the end of the battle the gun had a number of hits on it – but Pete was uninjured. He got nothing for his actions. Compare them to, say, the Bravo Two-Zero lads (which is not to say that they didn't deserve their decorations) and you will see how times have changed.

By the time of B Squadron's third tour in Oman in 1974, things were somewhat quieter. By this stage of the campaign a lot of the work was being done by Civil Action Teams and hard-core soldiering had taken a back seat – in comparison to Op Jaguar at any rate. The Adoo were feeling the squeeze by now, although they weren't beaten by a long chalk but, in any case, in recognition of my advancing years and distinguished service, I was given the role of squadron quartermaster sergeant at the SAS Headquarters at Um al Gwarif for part of it at least.

This wasn't a full-time post: when a big threat materialized against Salalah, we all took turns manning picket positions in the Jebel overlooking the coastal plain and the airfield; and they were getting hit on a regular basis (I still have a spent bullet somewhere that hit a sandbag just behind my head on one of these jobs) but it did mean that for a lot of the time I was out of the direct firing line.

There were still plenty of laughs to be had. On one occasion, a group of senior Firqa personnel showed up to collect some kit from Kevin Walsh. Kev had asked me to get everything set up for them but there was a little flurry of confusion and the squadron commander, Arish Turle, got involved. He was under the impression that we didn't have sufficient stores to give them what they needed and very apologetically told them, 'I'm very sorry, gentlemen, but we don't have the equipment you need right now. If you can come back next week, it will all be ready for you.'

Unfortunately, none of them spoke English.

'I say, Sergeant Walsh, would you mind translating that for me please.'

Kevin had just finished an Arabic course, so this shouldn't

have been too difficult for him. As Arish, Lofty Wiseman (the squadron sergeant major) and I watched benevolently, Kevin gathered them together in a half-circle. 'Come 'ere, gather round.' He now had their full attention. 'Listen: *ma'fee buckshees*.* Now fuck off!'

But being back at HQ meant that I was given the unpleasant task of escorting a mate of mine, Joe, to Colchester, the military prison in Essex. Joe had been sentenced to fifty-six days' detention for, let's say, showing a lack of judgement.

It was a very odd process. I had to get dressed up in full No. 2 dress, complete with beret and wings, and go from Hereford to Worcester where he was being held at the Light Infantry Barracks pending confirmation of sentence. Then I was handcuffed to him and we travelled by train, across country, to Colchester where we were picked up by a Land Rover at the station. We'd managed to have a bit of a laugh as we travelled down, but not surprisingly, as we got closer to Colchester, Joe's mood got a bit more sombre.

When we arrived at the guardroom, the first thing we heard was a bollocking being screamed at someone, followed by the stomp of hobnailed boots as a huge provost sergeant major emerged to see who we were. They were expecting Joe, of course, but I was a bit taken aback when having unlocked the handcuffs from Joe's wrist, the sergeant major marched me outside and began cobwebbing me round the square at high velocity.

'LEFT, RIGHT, LEFT, RIGHT, LEFT, RIGHT. LEFT...MARK TIME...LEFT, RIGHT, LEFT, RIGHT, LEFT, RIGHT, LEFT . . . QUICK MARCH. . . !'

Initially I assumed I was being taken to his office to fill out some paperwork. However, after about ten minutes of

---

* No freebies.

marching at triple time, I realized a mistake had been made.

I tried to interrupt. 'Sir, I . . .'

'SHADDAP! LEFT, RIGHT, LEFT, RIGHT, LEFT, RIGHT, LEFT . . .'

'Sir, I . . .'

'I SAID SHADDAP! MARK TIME! LEFT, RIGHT, LEFT, RIGHT, LEFT, RIGHT, LEFT . . .'

'SIR! I'M THE ESCORT!'

'HALT! What did you say?'

'Sir, I'm the escort, the other one's Corporal C——, the prisoner.'

'Why didn't you tell me, Corporal?'

'I tried, sir, but . . .'

'Never mind, come with me.'

We went back to the guardroom, where Joe was having a cup of coffee with some of the other provost staff.

'Are you Corporal C——?'

'Sir!'

'GET OUTSIDE AT THE DOUBLE! LEFT, RIGHT, LEFT, RIGHT, LEFT, RIGHT, LEFT . . .'

Poor Joe's arse didn't touch the ground. The sergeant major came back a few minutes later, while I was having a cup of coffee.

'I'm sorry about that, Corporal. Still, I expect you enjoyed the experience, didn't you?'

The reason he'd made the mistake was straightforward. At well over six feet himself, the sergeant major had looked at Joe, who was considerably taller than me and had G Squadron's red and blue Household Division backing behind his beret badge, and decided he couldn't possibly be the bad guy!

All I can say is, I might not be tall but at least I don't have the IQ of a flip-flop – and a left one at that.

CHAPTER SEVEN

As I said, the first time we dipped our toe into counter-terrorism was in Aden with Operation Nina, the so-called Keeni-meeni work in the town, when squads were sent in covertly with decoys to bring out terrorists and bring them to book, using the pistol and close-combat techniques developed by Alec Spence during the 1960s. But the role of the SAS in combating terrorism in Britain had yet to be defined. In that year, the new commanding officer, DLB, got one of the young officers, Captain Andy Massey, to make a study of possible SAS roles in counter-terrorism. Massey came up with the concept of the 'team', a self-contained assault force on permanent short-notice standby for deployment in case of hijackings, hostage takings and so forth, and this idea was 'staffed' through to the Ministry of Defence where it was shelved because of fears about using the army in police tasks.

It was a source of considerable concern at that time, when strikes and other industrial upheavals were commonplace, that the military should not be seen to be taking on any of the functions normally reserved for the police. 22 SAS had a clear role to play in fighting counter-insurgency campaigns but it was much less obvious that there was a need for some form of domestic assault force and, at that time, mainland

Britain had remained largely free from the kind of violence that might be countered by a military anti-terrorist force.

But Massey's ideas were soon revived. In September 1972 a group of Palestinian terrorists, from the so-called Black September group, attacked the Israeli team in their accommodation in the Olympic village in Munich, killing two and taking nine others hostage. The German authorities, utterly unprepared for such a situation, attempted to negotiate and then launched an ambush at Furstenwald airport, from which the terrorists and their hostages were about to be flown. In the chaos that followed, four Arab terrorists, one German policeman and all the Israeli hostages were killed. The operation was a complete fuck-up.

The shockwaves from Munich reverberated around the entire Western world. It was evident that very few, if any, domestic police forces were equipped, trained or psychologically prepared to deal with groups of well-organized terrorists armed with military weapons. In Britain, which already had a domestic counter-insurgency situation in Northern Ireland, Prime Minister Edward Heath's government turned to the Director of Military Operations for a solution. The DMO was immediately able to produce Massey's paper and authorization was granted to form a counter-terrorist team.

Well, this had to come from somewhere and in fact it turned out to be us in B Squadron. Starting from scratch, under the leadership of Lofty Wiseman, we began to put together what has since become 'the Team': the best-trained counter-terrorist force in the world.

But it wasn't all plain sailing. At the start all we had were pistols and SLRs as weapons – in other words, standard infantry equipment – while our vehicles were a selection of half and three-quarter ton Land Rovers, along with a couple of ropy old civilian Humbers, which we'd somehow acquired.

None of this was very satisfactory, and in the few weeks that we had available to acquire an operational anti-terrorist capability we made strenuous efforts to beef up our capability.

We were helped in the modernization and upgrading process by the airy promise of unlimited funds, given when the Regiment was first authorized to set up the team, under the codename 'Operation Snowdrop', and also by the arrival of Alec Spence, the close-quarter battle specialist, as the training guru. The money enabled us to buy some Range Rovers, then just coming on to the market, as our basic civilian type vehicle; while Alec made an assessment of our training requirements and weapons needs.

In the short term we got hold of a consignment of Ingram MAC-10 machine pistols, a compact but basic 9mm design which has since become popular amongst US-based drugs gangs, and which fulfilled our basic requirement at the time; and in the longer term this led to the testing and acquisition of a much wider range of weaponry as Alec and his newly created counter-revolutionary warfare cell defined the problems we would face in the course of counter-terrorist operations and then set about solving them. These included the Heckler and Koch family of sub-machine guns and rifles, Remington shotguns, stun grenades, the Arwen riot gun and an array of other weapons for specific tasks, ranging from low-profile 'bodyguarding' up to full-blown hostage rescue assaults. But, and it's a fairly big but, the techniques that were developed then are sensitive and remain secret for a good reason: the more they are discussed, the more terrorists can develop counter-measures. These things are so secret, that if I told you what they were, I'd have to come and kill you all afterwards; and at my age, with my dicky knee and back, that could take for ever.

But what we did do was swap techniques with allied teams that were set up at the same time. The Germans, after the Munich fiasco, were quick off the mark in setting up GSG-9 to prevent any further incidents, while the French came in with the GIGN, and the Americans, after a certain amount of um-ing and ah-ing, also created 'Delta Force' (Special Forces Operational Detachment Delta) in direct and conscious imitation of us, under Colonel Charlie Beckwith, a hugely experienced Vietnam veteran who had served in 22 SAS on attachment in the 1960s.

It is an acknowledged fact that counter-terrorist techniques are willingly shared between the democracies in order to maximize their chances of defeating this menace, and the Western world has become an enormously hostile environment for terrorists since 1972. This doesn't mean we don't get to laugh at each other. Snapper from B Squadron, one of the team that subsequently stormed the Iranian Embassy, was given the job of escorting a bunch of GSG-9 (the German anti-terrorist boys) to the 'Killing House' at the training area near Hereford. They trundled down there in a big charabanc, but as they arrived at the camp gates, the front tyre on the bus blew out and the whole thing lurched over in a kind of automotive stupor.

Snapper stood up at the front and told them, 'Sorry, lads, everybody off the bus. I'm afraid we'll have to walk from here.'

One of the Brussels* stood up and asked, 'How far iss ze range?'

'I'm afraid it's about three kilometres.'

'Vot about all ze assault eqvipment und veapons und ammunition?'

'I'm afraid we'll have to carry it.'

* Brussels sprouts = Krauts.

There was a certain amount of understandable moaning and griping as the Germans debussed, followed by the classic line as one blond stormtrooper disconsolately picked up his heavy body armour. 'How did zey vin ze var?'

The 'Killing House' was an actual house that we used to practise in - though being the SAS our role-playing was taken very seriously. The point, after all, is to learn how to deal with real terrorist situations and this can't be done if you're pussy-footing around.

Playing a terrorist was my least favourite role in these exercises. Even though I was fairly sure no one was going to stick a bullet in me, my adrenaline would start pumping at the sound of the team breaking in and clearing the house, room by room . . . I knew I was in for a certain amount of manhandling when they finally caught me and the sight of those big men dressed in black, faces hidden by gasmasks, was pretty intimidating. I couldn't see them smile as they recognized me but to show that they knew who I was, I'd often get a reassuring squeeze of the bollocks. They're a friendly lot, the SAS.

One time I took realism too far, though. On this particular exercise I had been appointed the role of chief terrorist, with a high-ranking army official as my hostage. He had been told to wear a gas mask for protection – but no one had told me this. So when the team threw the lot at us – gas, stun grenades – I did what any self-respecting ruthless terrorist would do. I grabbed the gas mask off my hostage and made my escape.

The team dragged him out of the house, red-faced with streaming eyes, and he calmed down eventually. I got a rocketing while G Squadron, safely round the corner, were collapsed with laughter.

Suffice to say that some of the skills we learnt were fairly strange and were not always used in the cause for which they were taught. I got back early from leave one Sunday evening and bumped into Jock from 16 Troop in the locker room as I was unpacking my gear. The Naafi was closed so we started to chat as he began to empty his suitcase into his locker, but we hadn't been there long when he made a kind of 'Ah hah!' sound, and produced a set of tools that he'd recently acquired whilst doing a Covert Methods of Entry course with the Intelligence Corps. He was showing me the contents when he suddenly said, 'Are you thinking what I'm thinking, Pete?'

'Almost certainly,' I told him.

So he started systematically going round the room, swapping the locks around. He got to the last one and stood back to survey his handiwork.

'That won't be enough, Jock, we've also got to change the name-cards.'

These are the little bits of cardboard that slip into a slot on the locker. We swapped them all.

Jock turned to me. 'That's still not enough, Pete.'

So we changed over all the rucksacks, webbing and other bits of kit that were stowed away on top of the lockers. Still not satisfied, we then physically moved all of the lockers around, so that even if they could still remember where it had been, the lads wouldn't be able to identify their own locker. By now we were knackered, but we were also in hysterics, waiting to see the lads' reaction when they returned.

As the boys began to arrive back on camp, Jock and I set up a discreet observation post at a window and waited for the fun. Sure enough, the whole billet was soon a mess of swearing, raging SAS troopers, surrounded by piles of other people's kit as they attempted to sort out the mess. At this point, it started to turn nasty. From our vantage-point, I heard big Brian Dodd saying, 'I bet fucking Scholey's behind this.'

There was general agreement. I reckoned I now had two choices: I could write out my will, or I could try to wriggle out of it. A thought occurred to me.

'Wait here, Jock, I'm going to the other window,' I whispered.

'Okay.'

I'd done some amateur theatricals and I reckoned it was time to collect my Oscar. I walked into the locker room and, before anyone could say anything, announced, 'Has someone been fucking around with your lockers? Mine's the same.'

Big Brian looked surprised. 'We thought you'd done it.'

'Not me, mate, it was fucking Jock. Look at him there, laughing at us through the window!'

I didn't need to be able to hear Jock to know what he was saying. 'You bastard, Scholey!'

He bolted, a fraction ahead of four members of his own troop.

In 1976 my twenty-two years regular service came up and I was faced with a choice: leave and try my hand at something new; or soldier on a little bit longer on continuance. Carolyn and I discussed it for some time, but in the end I decided to carry on. I was a bit over forty now, but I didn't feel ready for the knackers yet, and I still felt that I had something to offer the Regiment, even if I was no longer quite the lean, mean fighting machine I'd been when I'd first joined.

I now moved to operational research, the small team within the Regiment responsible for testing and assessing new equipment, and for developing our own stuff when we couldn't get hold of a commercial alternative. This was a cracking job, because it meant working with all the squadrons and departments within the Regiment, as well as a lot of outside agencies, including the police, the intelligence services and the various research and development departments belonging to the government.

It also meant a lot of liaison work with the Team and now, being effectively non-operational, us old lags in ops research did occasionally get roped in to help out with various forms of training. On one occasion I got detailed off to act as a hostage in one counter-terrorist team exercise. The scenario was that a group of terrorists – a regular army infantry platoon – had captured a group of hostages, including a VIP (me), and were holding us all in an old Victorian building.

These exercises always involve maximum realism: the commander is the actual chief constable of the area involved, they use a real negotiating team, and so on. This time, the terrorists' demands were not being met, so they decided that their VIP hostage was going to be executed to jolly things along a little. They gagged me, tied me up, 'shot' me and then shoved me out of a window. I rolled down a long, grassy bank, and finished up lying face down in the grass in the pouring rain for an hour and a half, whilst the team, from G Squadron, went through the drills and procedures before their assault.

I was lying there, looking forward to being untied and taken back to the holding area for a nice cup of tea, when four members of the team ran forward in their black assault gear. They lifted me shoulder high but instead of taking me back to 'safety' and the tea urn, they carried me up the grass bank and threw me back into the building, shouting at the terrorist inside, 'Have him back, he's a fucking creep!'

My boss in ops research was Lofty Wiseman, one of the great

characters of the SAS and also one of the key people who helped transform the Regiment into what it is today. Had his career prospects not been slightly dimmed when he had a set-to as squadron sergeant major with his squadron commander (I happened to be standing in the next door office and was surprised to see Lofty's huge fist come crashing through the wall as he took a wild swing at the officer in question), Lofty would almost certainly have ended up as quite a senior officer himself. In his time he helped reorganize the selection and training of SAS recruits, as well as putting in place the combat survival training for which he's since become well known, but he was an inspirational soldier and a really nice guy as well.

Some winters, heavy rains in Hereford would cause the Wye to break its banks and parts of the city would flood. On these occasions, the police would often ask for assistance from the Regiment and we would be found ferrying folk across a flooded area, using our amphibious craft.

On one occasion one street was completely cut off by the floods. It was a dark, cold miserable night with continuous rain. We got news of some old folk who were cut off and had been unable to get out to buy food for about two days or so. Lofty and his troop set out with rations and two large urns of tea on board an assault craft. Having given mugs of tea and sandwiches to a number of folk, he noticed an old lady about two storeys up looking out of the window. He somehow climbed from the craft up to her window with a big mug of tea. He went to hand it to her.

'Here you are, love,' he said to her, 'here's a nice warm mug of tea.'

'Has it got sugar in it?' she asked.

'Yes, it's lovely and sweet, do you the world of good.'

She looked at him hanging up there by the skin of his teeth and said, 'I don't take sugar.'

Lofty's philosophy of life was refreshingly straightforward. He was checking his passport in the orderly room one day when Angela Rose, the wife of Mike Rose, the CO, came in. Seeing Jakey, one of the troop corporals, doing some photo-copying, she asked whether he would be prepared to help put up a marquee at the weekend at one of the local schools for some public-relations event or other, and Jakey agreed. Then she spotted Lofty.

'Lofty, why doesn't your wife ever turn up to the Wives' Club events?'

Lofty gave it to her straight, tongue firmly in cheek. 'The thing is Angela, in my family, I'm the warrior. I go out and fight the wars, and my wife stays home and looks after my house and my seven kids.'

'Lofty, that's the most disgracefully chauvinistic thing I've ever heard! A woman can do anything a man can do and a lot more besides.'

Jakey was just leaving the office. 'You can put up your own bloody tent, then!'

It was also while I was in ops research that the Regiment was put on the map in a very big way. On 30 April 1980, a group of six Iraqi-sponsored terrorists arrived outside the Iranian Embassy building in Princes Gate in Knightsbridge, London. The six were ethnic Arabs from the oil-rich Iranian province of Khuzestan (also called Arabistan) which had been annexed by Iran in 1926; and the mainly Arabic population were undoubtedly the victims of persecution by the ethni-cally Persian authorities put in place above them. Nevertheless, it is most likely that the terrorists were agents of Iraqi intelligence, intent on causing trouble for the un-stable Islamic government of Iran.

After a brief struggle, the terrorist overpowered the Metropolitan Police guard, PC Trevor Lock, and took control of the building, seizing twenty-six hostages in the process. We initially got involved because 'Dusty' Gray, an ex-corporal from the Regiment, who had left to become a police dog-handler, phoned the ops room at Hereford and the Team actually began its move to London before a formal request had been made for SAS assistance. After a brief stopover at the army's language school in Beaconsfield, Red Team were deployed into a building close by the embassy in the early hours of 1 May and set to work on an Immediate Action option, a rough and ready plan for use in the event that the terrorists started killing their hostages before a deliberate assault plan could be developed.

As the siege dragged on Red Team were relieved by Blue at the embassy and headed for Regent's Park Barracks, where a mock-up of the embassy had been constructed by the Irish Guards pioneer section and they were able to work out their plans for a deliberate assault. In the meantime, Steve Callan and I were sent up from ops research to the embassy to set up various forms of covert surveillance gear that we were then experimenting with, including fibreoptic lenses which could be pushed through into the embassy itself to monitor what was going on. It was a tense and busy situation, and when we'd finished what we were doing, we packed up and went back to Hereford in order to keep out of B Squadron's way.

The crisis came to a head shortly after midday on 5 May. The terrorists had been assured by their controllers that they would be flying out of Britain with their hostages within twenty-four to forty-eight hours and were not psychologically prepared for a long siege. By day six they were extremely edgy and anxious: at 1240 their leader warned the police negotiators that he would start killing hostages in two hours' time but in fact the first shots were heard from inside just fifteen minutes later.

It seemed clear that someone had been shot, but a decision had been made at ministerial level that the SAS assault could only begin when *two* hostages had been killed because the first death might have been an accident. There was a delay whilst William Whitelaw, the Home Secretary, was briefed on the current military assessment by DLB, who had assumed control as Director SAS, and then the Team were brought up to immediate 'notice to move' (i. e., ready to go as soon as the order was given). This order was given (by the police commander at Princes Gate) at about 1550 and the assault team were declared ready at 1700, nearly an hour ahead of schedule. Thereafter, it was a question of waiting for developments. These were swift in coming.

At 1820, the police deployed a cleric from the Regent's Park mosque to talk to the terrorist leader, but whilst the conversation was in progress further shots were heard and shortly afterwards a body was dumped on the steps of the embassy. After permission had been given to remove it, a quick autopsy was carried out which swiftly established that the body (which was that of the embassy's press officer) had been dead for some hours. The logic of this discovery was that it was now possible, if not probable, that the required two hostages were dead. The police sought a decision from the home secretary, who in turn consulted Prime Minister Margaret Thatcher, and permission was given to send the SAS in on the orders of Assistant Commissioner John Dellow who was in command of the incident.

Once the decision had been made to use the military option, the aim of the negotiators shifted somewhat. At least part of their task now became to lull the terrorists into a false sense of security, and they sought to do this by agreeing to the terrorists' demand that they bring a bus to transport the terrorists and hostages to Heathrow Airport. In reality, as this was happening, the assault team was moving into position for the attack. The surviving recording of the negotiator talking to the terrorist leader culminates in the following sequence:

Salim (terrorist leader): We are listening to some suspicion . . . er . . . movements.
Negotiator: There are no suspicious movements.
Salim: There is suspicion, okay. Just a minute . . . I'll come back again . . . I'm going to check.

The sounds that Salim had heard were members of Red Team on the roof, preparing to abseil down the rear of the building, and a 'pair' from Blue Team placing a frame charge – designed by ops research – on the front window prior to scurrying back into cover. As Salim left the phone, the assault commander, Hector Gullan, gave the order 'Go! Go! Go!', and a large 'stun charge' in the embassy's lightwell was detonated. The explosion was audible halfway across London. Even so, the tape clearly shows the negotiator repeating *after the detonation*: 'Salim, there are no suspicious movements'!

It is not technically difficult to storm a single building like the Iranian embassy, but it is enormously difficult to storm such a building *and* rescue all or most of the hostages, and it was here that the long months of training paid off. In the first few seconds of the assault, one of the terrorists opened fire on the hostages, killing one of them, but very shortly afterwards the assault force had killed four of the terrorists and a fifth was shot by a sniper stationed in Hyde Park.

The sixth survived because he had downed tools and was no longer presenting a threat. As a result the lads were unable to positively identify him within the building and he was brought outside for arrest by the police.

Only one of the hostages died in the assault.

Things changed quickly after that. Apart from the fact that the Regiment was thoroughly in the spotlight all round the world, we'd become flavour of the month with the government as well. One of the most noticeable things that improved was pay: before 1980, you basically got paid one rank above the rank you held, and received parachute pay in addition. This actually meant that people like me, who were already getting parachute pay and held a rank, in my case corporal, lost money when they joined the Regiment because we dropped down to trooper. The upshot of this was that a lot of people used to moonlight when they were back in Hereford, working night shifts at local companies. Now we began to get a new allowance of Special Forces pay, which nearly doubled the pay of the troopers, and gave a big boost to the rest of us.

But despite this, I was beginning to think that it was time for me to move on. I'd stayed with the Regiment for so long because I loved the operational side of it but I had to recognize now that, in my early forties, I was getting too old for active involvement in operations. If the truth be told, I wasn't enjoying the operations and training so much either: there's a nasty moment in every soldier's life when lying in a ditch full of muddy water becomes a pain in the arse rather than a challenge, and as 1981 drew to a close, I decided that it was time to get out and make a fresh start.

EPILOGUE

I was in the process of becoming a sub-postmaster of all things, in Cheshire, when my nerve failed me. Driving up from Hereford with Carolyn in the early spring of 1982, I suddenly thought: I can't leave this town, and I can't leave this Regiment. It was almost as if I'd suddenly been stricken with homesickness. We had another long talk and agreed that I would stick with the army for the time being, and that she would go back to work, teaching special-needs children with behavioural disorders, when the children were older.

It was undoubtedly a difficult time for me: I'd been a soldier without a break since 1955, and I'd enjoyed almost every minute of those twenty-seven years. The time was coming when I would have to go, but faced with the immediate prospect of civilian life, I couldn't cut the cord that connected me to the army and the SAS.

And then, of all things, another war came along.

It was as much of a surprise to the SAS as it was to the rest of the British military and intelligence establishment when, on 1 April 1982, we discovered that Argentina was in the process of launching an invasion of the Falkland Islands, a rocky, windswept outpost of the former British Empire in the far South Atlantic.

In the confusion that followed, as the Task Force was hastily assembled, there was no clear thinking on how special forces might be employed and how many would be required, and it was at the initiative of the CO, Mike Rose, that D Squadron, under Cedric Delves, was despatched to the forward mounting base at Ascension Island, close to the Equator, on 4 April.

Rose went out the next day, taking a tactical SAS headquarters element, and soon linked up with Brigadier Julian Thompson, commander of 3 Commando Brigade, who was the land forces commander at the time. As a member of Thompson's planning staff, Rose was able to develop a special forces strategy which planned on using D Squadron in a raiding role, together with G Squadron in intelligence collection tasks.

The first difficulty to be overcome in the campaign stemmed from the unfamiliarity of the naval hierarchy with the potential scope and the type of support we needed for our operations. This was solved comparatively easily by establishing an SAS liaison cell within HQ Cincfleet in the bunker at Northwood, and by the personal intervention of DLB, who was still the Director SAS in 1982, and who ensured that the commander-in-chief, Admiral Fieldhouse, was fully briefed on SAS capabilities. The second difficulty was less tangible but, anecdotally at least, considerably more problematic: the chain of command and reporting. The full extent of the confusion over who was responsible for tasking special forces patrols at each stage in the campaign, and how the intelligence they acquired should be disseminated, wasn't ever completely resolved and the whole picture became crowded by inter-unit rivalries and jealousy based on a fear, I've always believed, that everyone thought this might be the last conventional war we'd ever fight.

The first operations in which we got involved were moves to recapture the island of South Georgia, 800 miles to the south-east of the Falklands group, which were held by a small force of Argentine commandos. South Georgia is a little over 105 miles long and approximately eighteen miles wide at its widest point, but its mountainous terrain and relative proximity to the Antarctic make it geographically and climatically a very different proposition from the Falklands, being icy and bleak, and scoured by severe winds carrying ice and snow particles at up to 100 miles an hour. For practical purposes, the island is uninhabited, apart from a small scientific team from the British Antarctic Survey, whose leader doubles as the island's magistrate and immigration chief.

It had been occupied by the Argentines on 3 April after a brief skirmish with a small party of about fifteen Royal Marines detached from the Falklands garrison at short notice, and landed from HMS *Endurance*.

The plan, developed in London, was to send a Royal Marines company (M Company of 42 Commando) together with an SBS section and a troop of SAS in a small Task Group consisting of the destroyer *Antrim*, the frigate *Plymouth*, and two auxiliaries, *Fort Austin* and *Tidespring*. The idea was that we would mount OPs providing information for the Marines who would then capture the enemy garrison with the assistance of naval gunfire support. The Argentine garrison was believed to be no more than about sixty strong, and to be based solely in the two tiny settlements of Grytviken and Leith (both former whaling stations), well out of range of land-based air cover, although a serious threat to the Task Group was present in the form of a submarine that was believed to be cruising the area.

The South Georgia Task Group left Ascension Island on 9 April for the voyage south with most of D Squadron embarked on the *Fort*, making intense preparations for their forthcoming operation.

The commander of the land element of the South Georgia Task Group was Major Guy Sheridan, the second-in-command of 42 Commando, but the SAS were placed under the command of the captain of *Antrim* who was the overall task Group commander. In reality, this meant that Cedric could act as his own boss – few naval officers would have sufficient experience or knowledge of special operations to question his decisions – but it led to D Squadron attempting an operation that came close to disaster: a helicopter insert onto a glacier.

Several people with experience of South Georgia thought that the heli-landing on the Fortuna glacier was a big mistake but, despite this, the SAS team, from 19 (Mountain) Troop under Captain John Hamilton, decided to go ahead. During the afternoon of 21 April, and after two abortive attempts, the troop bundled out of their helicopter and onto the glacier; the first British forces to return to the islands.

They soon realized that they had fucked up. The glacier was being buffeted by 50 m.p.h. winds that blew ice particles into their equipment and weapons and was criss-crossed by dangerous crevasses. They made about 500 metres in the first five hours' march, but then were obliged to seek shelter in a crevasse for the night. Having had a rethink they decided to request evacuation the next morning. This came in the form of three Wessex helicopters, of which two crashed in whiteout conditions without causing serious injury, before the last one got away, dangerously overloaded with the Mountain Troop boys.

A second attempt to land SAS soldiers was then made using the Boat Troop's Gemini inflatable motor-boats into Stromness Bay. This was similarly unsuccessful: three of the inflatables failed to start and had to be towed behind the two that did. Caught in a sudden squall, two of the unpowered boats broke free from their tows and were carried away. The crews of both were fortunate to be retrieved some time later after a few brown-trouser moments on the high seas.

As it turned out, the whole plan was somewhat over-elaborate. The end of the operation came when the Argentine submarine was spotted and rocketed by the *Endurance*'s helicopter, and D Squadron and the marines were then helicoptered ashore: the Argies bravely surrendered without firing a shot.

Meanwhile, back in Hereford, plans were afoot to mount a special operation on the Argentine mainland, and suddenly, Staff Sergeant Scholey found himself right back in the thick of it.

On 4 May the British destroyer HMS *Sheffield* was struck amidships by a French-built Exocet missile fired from a Super Étendard bomber of the Argentine naval air arm. In the ensuing explosion and fire, twenty members of the crew were killed and many more injured. The ship was abandoned and sank whilst under tow six days later.

The loss of the *Sheffield* had a huge impact on the Task Force and the war cabinet. The chiefs of staff had informed the cabinet that an amphibious landing, if it was to take place, needed to happen before 30 May, when the onset of the southern winter was likely to have made the weather too unpredictable, but the Super Étendard/Exocet threat appeared to be a potential war-loser even though the Argentines were known to have only a limited number of them. If an Exocet was to destroy one of the aircraft carriers or a troopship it might prevent the landings taking place at all. Some means, therefore, needed to be found to neutralize the Exocets. Various ideas were considered, and then rejected, before DLB managed to persuade Mrs Thatcher that he had the solution.

At the start of the Falklands campaign, B Squadron were put on standby as a strategic reserve for operations in the South Atlantic, under the command of John Moss, but there was a slight blip on the horizon in that Fred Marafono had just taken over from Jim Vakatalia as SQMS, but Fred had no experience of the 'Q' side of life. If B Squadron were deployed, they would certainly need an experienced hand in charge of the stores and resupply situation, so would Staff Sergeant Scholey mind lending a hand? He wouldn't mind at all.

But, to be fair, we didn't know what the plan was at that stage. We started doing a variety of different types of training: getting everybody up to speed on all the squadron weapons, working with helicopters and boats, practising signals procedures and all the hundred and one other things that need to be sorted out before we could deploy. I did some of the training but mostly I worked getting the squadron's equipment loaded and ready for the off.

But a few days after the *Sheffield* went down, we were summoned to the squadron interest room for a briefing. B Squadron was to launch an attack on an Argentinian airbase.

In essence, the concept was simple: two C-130 aircraft carrying B Squadron would take off from Ascension Island and fly, courtesy of air-to-air refuelling, across the South Atlantic ocean to Rio Grande where they would land and be abandoned. Once on the ground, B Squadron would fan out across the base, destroying as many Super Étendards and Exocet missiles as they could find and killing any Argentine aircrew that happened to be there. With the attack completed, B Squadron and their RAF aircrew would tactically evade across country, making for RVs.

We sat there gobsmacked. Then we started training. With a specific task in mind, I was now in a position to refine my stores loading, and we started to despatch material down to RAF Lyneham, pre-positioning it so that when we got the go-ahead, there would be no faffing about. Meanwhile, I was getting mildly concerned because, although the squadron were off doing mock attacks on airfields all round the country, I was still farting around with stores at Hereford. But if the squadron was going to do an attack then, as far as I was concerned, I was going to be part of it, and I needed to do the training as well. I tackled the SSM about this, and he told me that, as far as he was concerned, I was going, but that my first priority was to get the squadron's equipment sorted out, and I could join in with the specific operational training after that.

The guys had been training for ten days or so, and I was pretty much finished, when I got a call from the air movements people at Lyneham. There was a problem with our gear and could I help sort it out? I drove down in my old Maxi to see what the problem was and discovered that the two C-130s had been improperly loaded: the vehicles – Land Rovers and motorbikes – still had fuel on board; the explosives and ammunition were in the wrong places and the whole lot needed to be unloaded then reloaded safely. They were certainly in no state to fly and the RAF would refuse to try anyway.

About this time, a convoy with more kit on turned up from Hereford, together with eight drivers: six from the RCT and two civvies. When they'd finished unloading, I grabbed them all and said, 'Sorry, lads, you've got to stay here with me. If we don't sort out these C-130s, B Squadron aren't going anywhere.' To my surprise, there wasn't a murmur of protest, even though they were in for a huge amount of work. I turned to the two civvies and told them, 'You two had better head on back.'

'Don't worry, Pete, we can give you the rest of the day as well.' I was amazed. I phoned Dave Handley, the MTO, to clear it with him, and was told, 'Don't worry, Pete, you do what you've got to do.'

I sorted the drivers out with a meal in the cookhouse and accommodation and we got down to it, under the direction of an RAF air loadmaster. After two days of hard graft, we were finished and I phoned in to report that everything was ready.

'You'd better get back here, Pete, things are moving,' I was told. I finished a few final details and drove back to Hereford. It was strangely quiet. I went to the B Squadron office to find it empty. They'd gone and left me behind. A few phone calls confirmed that there was no chance I could catch them up: they were already on their way to Ascension Island.

Thus it was that I missed the last tumultuous days before B Squadron left. I knew that some people in the squadron weren't happy about the mission and, on the face of it, it looked very dicey, but I was surprised to learn what had happened. DLB had turned up at a squadron briefing (wearing his jumper the wrong way round, oddly enough) and, during the questions, had been asked why there was no air cover for the operation. His answer wasn't terribly reassuring.

'We wanted to take a couple of Phantoms, but we think they would probably be shot down by Argentine air defences.'

Boss Moss pulled a funny face at that. It was obvious what he was thinking: If they're going to take out Phantoms, what are they going to do to a pair of C-130s? Discussion became slightly heated, at which point DLB more or less ended the debate by stating, 'The bottom line is: B Squadron or the Fleet.'

DLB was pretty taken aback by the squadron's reaction to his plan and was even more surprised when one of the staff sergeants voluntarily resigned rather than take part in what he regarded as a suicide mission. During the night before they went, Boss Moss was replaced by Ian Crooke, so it was a pretty shell-shocked squadron that departed for Ascension Island without me.

Meanwhile, the war was continuing. G Squadron were inserted onto the Falklands to set up their OP matrix, whilst D Squadron launched a completely successful attack on an Argentine airfield at Pebble Island off West Falkland, where they'd dispersed a lot of their important Pucara ground-attack aircraft. Staff Sergeant Scholey, on the other hand, went home to wait and see what happened.

Two days after the squadron had left I had a feeling something was wrong and I decided to go onto camp to see what was going on. When I arrived, I could see that something was up: there were a lot of people bustling around, and I was told that there was a briefing for all personnel in the lecture room in thirty minutes. I knew then it was something awful. It was. A Sea King helicopter had gone down, taking twenty-two people with it, the majority of whom were members of D and G Squadrons, including both SSMs: Akker Atkinson from G Squadron, and Lawrence Gallagher from D . . .

The war came to an end three weeks later with only one further SAS casualty, John Hamilton, 19 Troop's commander. B Squadron never did get to launch their operation: the arrival of a radar guardship near to their target persuaded the powers-that-be that it was not going to work and instead they began to examine the options for a similar attack on Port Stanley airfield. In the end, that was binned as well, and elements of the squadron flew down to the islands just in time for the surrender.

It was also, finally, the end of the road for me. After we'd tidied up the squadron and brushed it down, I handed the stores over to Fred. I was forty-six now, and I'd been with the SAS for the best part of twenty years, and it was time to leave. I could have stayed, but it would have been doing a crap nothing-job like running the sergeants' mess bar, and that would have been a miserable way to end my career. I put my notice in, and I left.

But, of course, a career change at the age of forty-six is not the easiest thing to do. I had my pension but I also had two young children to support (Amy and David: born despite expert opinion that we'd never be able to have kids), and although my wife had her teaching job, we were accustomed to being a two-income family.

In the end, I started working on what is loosely called the circuit: bodyguarding a variety of VIPs of one sort or another, ranging from Mohammed al Fayed (briefly) to Cliff Richard, who is a very nice man. I also acquired the contract to run the security operation for the Miss World competition, the story of which would make a book in itself.

Whatever people like to claim, bread and butter bodyguard work isn't very interesting and isn't very well paid, and there are far too many people – some of whom have no conceivable qualifications for the job – chasing far too few contracts. When I first started out there were undoubtedly lean times but things improved over the years, and I've now reached a stage where I can work if I want to, but I'm secure enough not to have to.

As a sideline, my friend Mark Howarth and I also started to run leadership courses, under the name Black Knight, for schools, businesses and cadet forces units. I also work as a guest instructor for Colin Wallace's very successful Team Dynamics courses. So, all in all, things have worked out very well for me. I've survived, after all, to live in comfortable semi-retirement when many former comrades didn't: Paddy was killed in a car accident and Kevin succumbed to a tumour and so many other old friends have died young. They are never far from my thoughts. Whenever Lofty Wiseman, Don Large and I get together for a couple of beers we find ourselves chuckling over the exploits of Kev, the airborne wart, in particular.

There is no great moral to my life: I did the things I did because I enjoyed them; I liked the excitement; and I liked the people I worked with. The SAS was a tremendous organization to be part of, and I'm very proud to have been a member of it, but so was the Parachute Regiment, the Royal Artillery and the RASC. The British Army is far and away the most effective armed force, man for man, in the world; and we've achieved that without inflicting atrocities on civilians and non-combatants in campaign after campaign.

Throughout my military career, people saw me as a clown: well, I did muck about a bit, but when it mattered, I did the job and did it properly. In any case, no matter how you shuffle the cards, there's always a joker in the pack somewhere.

GLOSSARY

.303 The standard British Army rifle calibre from 1897 to 1958. A hugely powerful and accurate bullet, it is still encountered in some armies in the developing world.

44 pattern A type of canvas webbing equipment specially designed for jungle warfare and introduced in the British Army in 1944.

58 pattern The general issue webbing equipment in use by British forces since the early 1960s.

66 A light, portable, American-made, hand-held anti-tank rocket of 66mm nominal calibre and a maximum range of 200 metres. When fired accurately (no mean achievement), the 66 was found to have an impressive effect on static positions.

9mm The ammunition calibre used by British forces in pistols and sub-machine guns. '9mm' is also the generic term in the army for the Browning Hi-Power pistol issued to some personnel.

Adjutant An officer, normally of the rank of captain, who acts as the commanding officer's 'right-hand man' in peace and war, with special responsibility for personnel and discipline.

Advance to Contact A form of operation in which a unit, or sub-unit, travels along a set route until it meets an enemy position which it then engages. Normally used when the precise location of the enemy is unclear.

Armalite A 5.56mm light automatic rifle of American design used by the SAS since the mid-1960s, also known as the AR-15 and M16.

Bandolier A green plastic pouch issued to hold belts of 7.62mm machine-gun ammunition. An unpopular and fiddly item, the majority of soldiers prefer to carry belted ammunition slung around their bodies.

Basha An improvized shelter, normally constructed from the rainproof nylon poncho issued to all soldiers. In the SAS it is the generic term for all accommodation buildings.

Battalion A military unit typically composed of between 500 and 1000 soldiers commanded by a Lieutenant Colonel.

Belt-kit Webbing equipment adapted to be worn without a shoulder harness or yoke. In the British army it suggests membership of a Special Forces or specialist patrol unit.

Bergan The generic term in the British army for any military-type rucksack.

Beverley A British STOL transport aircraft of the 1950s and 1960s.

Brigade A military formation comprising two, or more, battalions and commanded by a . . .

Brigadier A 1-Star general of the British army or Royal Marines.

C-130 A 4-engined turbo-prop driven aircraft used as a general transport and Paratroop drop aircraft.

Captain Junior officer in the British army, typically employed on the battalion staff or as a company second-in-command. In 22 SAS, captains are employed as troop commanders.

Carl Gustav An 84mm anti-tank rocket launcher of Swedish design.

Chinook Large twin-rotor transport helicopter which can transport up to half a company of infantry.

CO Commanding officer. Normally a lieutenant colonel, a CO in the British army commands a unit of battalion-size or its equivalent.

Combats Generic army term for the heavy-duty camouflaged clothing worn in the field.

Company A sub-unit of an infantry battalion, normally comprising about 100 men commanded by a major. Equivalent-sized units of other arms are squadrons, batteries etc.

Compo Generic term for field rations issued by the British Army.

Corporal A junior non-commissioned officer, often to be found commanding a section of eight or ten men or a four-man patrol in the SAS.

CQMS (or SQMS) Company/squadron quartermaster sergeant. Appointment normally filled by a staff/colour sergeant, the CQMS is responsible for channelling stores from the quartermaster's department to his company, and for controlling their issue.

Crap-Hat (or 'hat') Any soldier who does not wear the maroon beret of airborne forces.

Crow A newly-joined, inexperienced soldier.

CSM (or SSM) Company/squadron sergeant major. A warrant officer class 2 who acts as right-hand man to a company or squadron commander. In battle, the CSM's task is to organise ammunition resupply for his fighting soldiers. In 22 SAS the SSMs are enormously influential figures and it is not unheard of for them to fulfil the squadron commander's appointment in the absence of a suitable officer.

D-day The specific day on which an operation takes place.

Det. Abbreviation of detonator.

DF A specific location onto which pre-arranged artillery fire can be brought.

Division A military formation comprising two, or more, brigades, and commanded by a Major General.

DMS Direct moulded sole, cheaply made, rubber-soled ankle boots issued by the British Army from the 1960s to the mid-1980s.

Dog-tags Metal discs worn by all soldiers in combat as a means of identifying their bodies afterwards. They bear the owner's name, number, religion and blood-group.

Doss-bag Military slang for sleeping-bag.

DPM Disruptive pattern material. British-pattern camouflaged cloth.

DZ Drop Zone

Endex 'End of Exercise'. Used on completion of virtually every task.

Exocet Effective French-built anti-ship missile used to devastating effect by the Argentine navy during the Falklands War.

Field Dressing Sterile pad with attached bandages issued to soldiers for emergency first aid in the field.

Firqat 'Company of men' (Arabic). Militia units raised and trained by 22 SAS during Operation Storm.

FOO Forward observation officer. Artillery officer, normally a lieutenant or captain, who accompanies infantry troops and brings in aimed artillery fire onto targets at their request or on his own initiative.

FPF Final protective fire. A high-priority DF used as a last resort very close to a friendly position if it appears likely to be overrun.

Gazelle A light reconnaissance helicopter.

Goon Troop Soldiers who have failed SAS selection by a narrow margin who remain at Hereford for a second attempt.

GPMG A belt-fed 7.62mm machine gun (also known as a gympy).

Green Slime Members of the Intelligence Corps attached to 22 SAS.

Headshed An SAS term for the commanding officer.

H Hour The specific time at which an operation starts.

HE High explosives.

Illum Starshells and flares used to light up a battlefield.

IO Intelligence officer. A member of the battalion staff - normally a captain or senior lieutenant - responsible for disseminating intelligence reports to the CO and company commanders, and reporting intelligence information to superior formations. In 22 SAS it is an officer from the Intelligence Corps.

IWS Individual weapon sight. A bulky nightsight that can be mounted on a rifle or machine gun, or used like a telescope.

Jebel Arabic for mountains.

Kevlar A fabric developed for the US space programme which has proved resistant to low-velocity bullets and shrapnel. Now used in body armour and helmets.

Lance Corporal The first rung on the promotion ladder for soldiers. Often carries with it the appointment of second-in-command of a section of eight men.

Larkspur Tactical VHF radio system superseded by the vastly superior 'Clansman'.

Lieutenant Junior officer with at least two years service (unless a university graduate). Will generally be commanding a platoon of 30 men.

Lieutenant Colonel A senior officer, normally commanding a regiment or battalion-sized unit or holding a senior staff appointment.

Lieutenant General A 3-star general under the British system, may command a Corps.

Major A 'field' grade officer, often commanding a squadron, company or equivalent-sized sub-unit.

Major General A 2-star general, often commanding a division.

Milan A wire-guided anti-tank missile with a range of up to 1950 metres.

Mirage A French-built fighter bomber used by the Argentines during the Falklands conflict.

MO Medical officer.

Morphine In combat, soldiers are issued with a dose of morphine-based painkiller to use on themselves if they are wounded. It comes in the form of a 'syrette', a small tube with attached hypodermic needle, for intramuscular injection.

MT Mechanical transport.

MTO Mechanical transport officer, an appointment usually held by an officer newly commissioned from the ranks.

ND Negligent discharge (of a weapon). An ND is a serious occurrence in the British Army; aside from being highly dangerous, it is indicative of sloppy drills and lack of professionalism.

NOD Night observation device.

O Group The O group is the means by which detailed operational orders are passed down the chain of command. It is, necessarily, a formal event which is usually carefully stage-managed and controlled by the commander giving the orders. The sequence of events is as follows: the commander describes the ground over which the operation he is outlining will take place and follows this with a briefing on the situation (the intelligence picture, what 'friendly forces' are doing, who is attached and detached for the operation, etc); once the situation has been described, the commander must then give a clear and simple mission statement (for example: 'to capture Mount Longdon'); at this point, the commander gives an outline of his plan and then goes on to describe in detail what he wants of each individual sub-unit under his command, this is followed by co-ordinating instructions explaining such crucial matters as timings; these are followed by a round up of essentially administrative points, and signals instructions. The formal structure and set format of an O group should mean that subordinate commanders will not miss any relevant orders or instructions.

OC Officer Commanding. The formal title of an officer in charge of a unit smaller than a battalion (i.e. a squadron, company, troop or platoon).

OP Observation post.

Ops Officer Operations officer. The battalion ops officer is responsible for the co-ordination and administration of the battalion's operational tasks and for assisting the CO in his planning process.

P Company P Company is a set of physical tests designed to assess an individual soldier's aptitude for serving with airborne forces. It occupies the most gruelling week of a Para recruit's basic training.

Padre All infantry battalions and most other major units have an attached chaplain known as the padre. Although padres are given officer's rank, they do not use it when dealing with soldiers to whom they are expected to provide spiritual leadership and moral guidance.

Patrol The four-man team which is the building block of SAS operations.

PC Platoon commander.

Platoon Sub-unit of an infantry company, normally comprising about thirty men commanded by a lieutenant or second lieutenant.

Pucara Argentine-built turbo-prop bomber designed for counter-insurgency and close air support applications.

QM Quartermaster. The officer, normally commissioned through the ranks, who is responsible for the battalion's logisitics.

R Group Reconnaissance group. A small team led by the CO, normally including the adjutant, a signaller and some bodyguards, which may leave the battalion tactical HQ in order to allow the CO to make a personal assessment of the battlefield situation.

RAP Regimental aid post. Battalion-level casualty clearing station where the wounded of both sides are assessed, stabilized and prepared for evacuation.

REMF Rear echelon mother fucker. A non-combatant soldier.

RSM Regimental sergeant major.

RSO Regimental signals officer.

RTU Returned to unit.

RV Rendevous.

Sangar A defensive position constructed above ground using sandbags, earth, peat or rocks, as opposed to a trench which is dug into the ground.

SAS Special Air Service. A multi-roled Special Forces unit of the British army. The majority of its members are recruited from the Parachute Regiment.

SBS Special Boat Squadron. A special forces unit recruited from the Royal Marine Commandos, with particular skills in amphibious and underwater infiltration of their targets. Now expanded, it is called the Special Boat Service.

Sea King Troop carrying helicopter in service with the Royal Navy.

Second Lieutenant The most junior officer's rank. A second lieutenant will normally be in command of a platoon.

Section A sub-unit of a platoon, normally comprising eight to ten men commanded by a corporal.

Sergeant Senior NCO, normally employed as second-in-command of a platoon or troop.

SLR Self Loading Rifle. Semi-automatic British variant of the fully-automatic 7.62mm FN FAL.

SMG Submachine-gun. A small fully-automatic weapon which normally fires pistol ammunition. In the British Army, this meant the 9mm Sterling-Patchett carbine.

SQMS see CQMS.

Staff Sergeant Also known as a 'colour sergeant' in the infantry. Senior NCO, usually employed as SQMS or sometimes as a troop commander.

Super Étendard French-made naval fighter-bomber. Capable of carrying the air-launched version of the Exocet missile.

Tab Tactical advance into battle. Paras slang for a forced march ('like yomping only faster and harder').

Team, the The SAS counter terrorist team.

Tom Any private soldier in the Paras.

Troop A 16 man sub-unit of 22 SAS nominally commanded by a Captain but in fact usually led by a staff sergeant.

Webbing The green canvas belt, harness and pouches used to carry ammunition water and other essentials into battle. Also known as 'fighting order', 'belt-kit' and 'belt order'.

Wetrep Weather report.

Windproof High-quality camouflaged combat jacket.

Wombat 120mm recoilless anti-tank gun issued at battalion level. Superseded by the Milan system.

Zulu time Greenwich Mean Time. Used in all military operations in order to avoid confusion.

INDEX

239